...p Kaufman |

Contemporary Film Directors

Edited by James Naremore

The Contemporary Film Directors series provides concise, well-written introductions to directors from around the world and from every level of the film industry. Its chief aims are to broaden our awareness of important artists, to give serious critical attention to their work, and to illustrate the variety and vitality of contemporary cinema. Contributors to the series include an array of internationally respected critics and academics. Each volume contains an incisive critical commentary, an informative interview with the director, and a detailed filmography.

A list of books in the series appears
at the end of this book.

Philip Kaufman |

Annette Insdorf

UNIVERSITY
OF
ILLINOIS
PRESS
URBANA,
CHICAGO,
AND
SPRINGFIELD

Frontispiece: Philip Kaufman, New York, December 1993.
Photo courtesey of Robert A. Ripps, © 2012.

Library of Congress Cataloging-in-Publication Data
Insdorf, Annette.
Philip Kaufman / by Annette Insdorf.
p.   cm. — (Contemporary film directors)
Includes bibliographical references and index.
Includes filmography.
ISBN 978-0-252-03685-9 (hardcover : alk. paper) —
ISBN 978-0-252-07846-0 (pbk. : alk. paper) —
ISBN 978-0-252-09397-5 (e-book)
1. Kaufman, Philip, 1936–
—Criticism and interpretation.
I. Title.
PN1998.3.K3828I58   2012
791.4302'33092—dc23   2011034120

Dedicated to the memory of two formidable women:
Rose Kaufman and my mother, Cecile Insdorf

Contents

Acknowledgments |

What a pleasure it is for a professor to quote her students' papers! Like my book on Krzysztof Kieslowski, this analysis is informed by the sympathetic understanding of dozens of Columbia University undergraduates as well as MFA candidates who studied Kaufman's work with me. In addition to the ones cited in my extended critical essay, I thank Ali Sargent for her sharp questions, Nick Carr for his help with photos, and Robert Brink for his critical as well as technological savvy. I appreciate the support of my agent Georges Borchardt as well as Barbara Galletly, and the confidence of the Contemporary Film Directors editor, James Naremore. I thank Joan Catapano and Daniel Nasset at University of Illinois Press. I am pleased to acknowledge that parts of this book appeared previously in *Tin House* 2.2 (Winter 2001): 289–99 (about *The Unbearable Lightness of Being*) and movingimagesource.us (a reappraisal of *Invasion of the Body Snatchers* in June 2008).

   I have been exceedingly lucky to find a subject as generous as Philip Kaufman, whom I have been interviewing for almost twenty years: he and his son Peter made countless materials available to me. They exemplify something that I feel keenly: family matters. For this book, as with most things, my husband Mark Ethan Toporek has been my anchor, a wise and loving partner.

Philip Kaufman

An Eye for an "I"

Philip Kaufman's cinema is stylistically and philosophically rich, but he has not received the kind of acclaim routinely showered on his peers. One reason is that the movies of directors such as Woody Allen, Robert Altman, or Quentin Tarantino are easier to categorize as belonging to one person. Because Kaufman's versatility is greater than his recognizability, he is considered less of an auteur. But close analysis of his twelve films reveals a true auteur at work. They are connected first by formal majesty: if Flaubert invoked "le mot juste" (the exact word), Kaufman finds "l'image juste"—the precise cinematic device appropriate to the story. Second, they are linked by an exploration of recurring and resonant themes. No other living American director has so consistently and successfully made movies for adults, tackling sensuality, artistic creation, and manipulation by authorities (governmental as well as technological).

His adaptations demonstrate that Kaufman is equal parts master craftsman and humanist. For example, despite their wildly different source material, *The Right Stuff*—which, according to Tarantino, "created a new genre, the hip epic" (qtd. in Barra 70)—and *The Unbear-able Lightness of Being* work on at least two levels: each tells the story of compelling individuals pushing the envelope in a vivid place and time, and each finds a uniquely appropriate cinematic vocabulary for the tale. Kaufman thus invites us to reflect on the very process of visual story-telling at the same time that he weaves the complex interactions of the individual body and the social landscape. As he told the critic Terrence Rafferty, "For me, the fun is in the learning experience, in figuring out the vocabulary you need for each movie. Every time it's like traveling to a new country, almost like a pilgrimage" (216). Whereas the "I" of the authorial voice dominates many of the books that serve as inspiration for his films, Kaufman's cinematic "eye" translates them into sensuous mo-tion pictures. When his characters engage in pleasurable erotic activity, the camera invites our own voyeurism; but when they are captured by surveillance monitors, a discomfiting identification with control expresses his anti-authoritarian stance. In Kaufman's films, what voyeurism is to pleasure, surveillance is to control. Unlike voyeurism, surveillance denies privacy or intimacy. If the erotic gaze is strongest when shared by the subject and object, surveillance depends upon an imbalance of power between the one who controls the gaze and its unwitting object.

This book grows out of a seminar I taught at Columbia University in the spring 2002 semester, "Auteur Study: Philip Kaufman," which in turn led to a number of other seminars devoted to his work. My students and I watched each of his films—usually twice—with the kind of attention they deserve, thereby noticing thematic and stylistic continuities. The advent of VHS and DVD technology serves a director like Kaufman even more than others: almost always richer on second or third viewing, his movies are layered, fulfilling my criteria for cinematic greatness: coher-ence and resonance. They exemplify François Truffaut's claim, "For me, a movie should express both an idea of the cinema and an idea of the world" (17). The density of detail led me to send weekly emails to the director, asking questions posed by the class. Since he replied, graciously and candidly, the quotations throughout the book—unless otherwise noted—are from this email correspondence (which spans subsequent classes, from spring 2002 through May 2011).

Given that there is no book-length study of Kaufman's cinema, this one covers each of his films—via a thematic approach—beginning with his first movies, *Goldstein* and *Frank's Greatest Adventure* (also known as *Fearless Frank*). The greatest attention is paid to his masterpiece, *The Unbearable Lightness of Being*, which—along with *Henry and June* and *Quills*—examines sensual and artistic freedom. As Manohla Dargis perceptively puts it, "While Kaufman remains best known for his astronaut saga *The Right Stuff*, he's demonstrated an unusual gift, particularly for an American director, for inflaming an audience's libido without doing insult to its intelligence" (198). His cinematic treatment of male relationships and codes of honor is examined in *The Great Northfield Minnesota Raid*, *The White Dawn*, *The Wanderers*, and *The Right Stuff*. Kaufman's exploration of deceptive images is traced from *Invasion of the Body Snatchers* to *Rising Sun* and *Twisted*.

Kaufman is hard to pin down: a visual stylist who is truly literate, a San Franciscan who often makes European films, he is an accessible storyteller with a sophisticated touch. But there are great rewards to be found in his vigorous, sexy, and reflective cinema. Like the subjects of my two previous auteur studies, Truffaut and Kieslowski, Kaufman displays affection for characters, actors, and spectators, challenging them to behave with intelligence, courage, and tenderness. Thierry Frémaux described the Lumière Institute's tribute to Kaufman in 2000 as "[t]he retrospective of a beautiful oeuvre, built by a discreet auteur who has made powerful and always unique films" (3).

Origins

Born in Chicago in 1936, Philip Kaufman met Rose Fisher, his future wife and writing partner, at the University of Chicago. He attended Harvard Law School for a year (where he saw and was thrilled by *The Seventh Seal*) and returned to the University of Chicago to work on a graduate degree in history. But instead of writing his master's thesis, he moved with Rose and their infant son Peter to the San Francisco Bay area in 1960. The Kaufman family took off for Europe precisely when the French New Wave was rising, and its giddy sense of experimentation made quite an impression. In Greece, he taught English; in Florence, he taught math. It was in Italy that he saw John Cassavetes's seminal independent American film *Shadows* and later—in a movie theater near Amsterdam—Shirley Clarke's *The Connection*. As he recalled, "Those

Philip, Peter, and Rose Kaufman, Berkeley 1968. In *The Unbearable Lightness of Being,* Teresa develops this photo as if she took it in Prague. Courtesy of Peter Kaufman.

two movies were for me the start of something new here—I could feel the cry of America, the sense of jazz. Then there were inklings of what became known for a brief period of time as the New American Cinema. So I came back to Chicago in 1962 and set about trying to learn as much as I could, seeing every foreign movie I could" (qtd. in Cowie 115). Kaufman would learn to become a director by turning his unfinished novel into *Goldstein,* an American independent "nouvelle vague" hybrid. And his subsequent work continued to manifest European inspiration as well as sophistication.

Goldstein and *Fearless Frank*

> When we saw *Les 400 coups*, just the vitality, and the children, and the camera being out in the streets, blew us away. It was the combination of technique and content that was so impressive: that accessibility.
>
> —Philip Kaufman on Truffaut's first feature

After films like *The Right Stuff* and *The Unbearable Lightness of Being*, we associate Kaufman with serious themes and visual sophistication. However, his first two features—*Goldstein* (1964) and *Frank's Greatest Adventure* (1967)—are larks, filled with youthful experimentation. If his later work suggests the influence of Akira Kurosawa, these breezy movies are more redolent of Federico Fellini, not to mention fairy tales, Jewish fables, and comic strips. *Goldstein*, which he cowrote and codirected with Benjamin Manaster, is inspired by a story from Martin Buber's *Tales of the Hasidim*. Kaufman initially conceived it as a novel, but—at the urging of Anaïs Nin—turned his unfinished book into what he called a "mystical comedy." Starring members of Chicago's famed Second City comedy troupe, it won the New Critics Prize at the 1964 Cannes Film Festival (shared with another auspicious first feature, Bernardo Berto-lucci's *Before the Revolution*). Its freewheeling tone reveals Kaufman's affection for John Cassavetes, the French New Wave, Jean Renoir, and Vittorio de Sica.[1] As in their films, the sense of place is authentic, rooted in Chicago rather than redolent of a studio.

An old codger (Lou Gilbert) with a wooden staff emerges from Lake Michigan. (Although he is never named, we will call him Goldstein.) A woman (Ellen Madison) is told by an antic doctor (Del Close) that she is pregnant; establishing the film's black comic tone, he says, "You blew it." A sculptor (Tom Erhart) uses destroyed car parts for his creations. Goldstein is chased in a sausage factory, where his pursuer farcically ends up as raw material for the mass-produced sausages. On a moving truck with the sign, "Goldstein's Paint and Glass," the petulant old man throws everything onto the highway. The pregnant woman undergoes an extended abortion performed by fools (a bold scene for 1964, nine years before *Roe v. Wade*), while the sculptor and another tall man (Ben Carruthers, from Cassavetes's 1960 *Shadows*) run looking for Goldstein, to the accompaniment of lively Klezmer music. Ben dances with tasseled women in a club, and Goldstein does a Hasidic dance with his shadow along a beach. The sculptor keeps running—searching for Goldstein while holding a staff, among trees—but the old man has disappeared, leaving only his hat on shimmering water. The sculptor finally collapses in the foliage, apparently happy in nature.

Goldstein opens with two elements that will become central to Kaufman's cinematic storytelling: the gaze and voiceover narration. Behind a tree branch, an eye opens, as a male narrator intones, "Every man is a tree in the wilderness with no one to rely on save for. . . ." It is an obscured shot that conceals as much information as it reveals. From this point on, *Goldstein*—like Kaufman's subsequent films—unfolds on the double axis of visual and oral self-consciousness. The upbeat music (credited to Meyer Kupferman) is part of a Klezmer-inflected sound, centered first on trumpet and later on violin, accordion, flute, drums, and oboe. The second shot withholds sound as we see a tall man and a woman. Then we hear their conversation as a voiceover in a museum. Sound and image are no more harmonious than in Jean-Luc Godard's early work. Like his *Vivre sa vie* (1962), *Goldstein* often presents sound recorded so "realistically" that we cannot discern the dialogue—for example, when Ben talks to the pregnant woman at a crowded bar. Later, Goldstein repeats the last word of other people's sentences. (His child-like repetition anticipates the mimicry of *Invasion of the Body Snatchers*.) And, at the end, there is a curious repetition of a woman's giggle and "thank you" after Ben (wearing sunglasses and a cap, resembling Jean-Paul Belmondo in *Breathless*) gives dollar bills to various exotic dancers. Sound cannot be taken for granted, especially when the same conversation continues as a voiceover in a surreal loop. This constitutes part of the film's absurdist humor, which includes the nondiegetic sound of a crash after we see a plane about to land (bringing the abortionists to Chicago).

Comic elements abound visually as well, like the meal set on the table in the first home Goldstein visits: on each plate is a wrapped loaf of bread. The iris on "Elijah" emerging from Lake Michigan is a kind of eye winking that continues with Goldstein urinating in the street: the sound turns out to be from an open fire hydrant. This playful disconti-nuity is developed when Goldstein pushes a hefty guy in a wheelchair who is playing the violin—but only pretending to make the music we are hearing. (Although they interrupt a funeral procession, there is a comical shot of a couple necking in the back seat of one of the cars.) When Goldstein takes a hot bath in the "violinist's" home, his connection to water is heightened. Later, he sips from a plate in a restaurant, blows his nose extensively, and ends up in the shimmering lake. Water is indeed the very structure of the film, a flow rather than a dramatically coherent construct.

The elemental imagery of *Goldstein* contains—in addition to water—numerous trees (and Goldstein's wooden staff), as well as the sculptor's flames (cross-cut with the ocean). The sparks from the sculptor's artwork are visually rhymed by the birds flying over the water, which link the sculptor and the old man before his emergence. This contributes to the mythic aspect of the film, what Kaufman called "the Buberesque traditional fable of the Prophet Elijah, roaming the world as a hobo, a bum, searching for an honest man. The baton is passed on to the young man who goes off after him at the end, looking for what is lost—probably becoming one of the thirty-six hidden *tzaddiks*. We leave the empty chair for the Prophet Elijah, hoping he'll come back again and make a sequel to *Goldstein*."

The camera's frequent tracking expresses Kaufman's themes of mobility and freedom (as opposed to the static camera in the upper-class home of the sculptor's father). *Goldstein* is consequently reminiscent of *Boudu Saved from Drowning* (1932), although Kaufman saw Jean Renoir's film only after making his own. Each centers on a tramp who emerges from water and wreaks havoc, leading to comic as well as criminal incidents. Both Boudu (Michel Simon) and Goldstein reject material possessions, as when Kaufman's protagonist throws items off the moving truck. And both directors depict levels of creation: *Goldstein* shows not only the making of sausages and the unmaking of a baby's birth but the shaping of art. If we feel raw material and energy rather than completed masterpieces, it is perhaps because these filmmakers are more concerned with the process than the result; as the sculptor says about searching for the Elijah figure, "It's not finding him. I'm gonna look for him." (The camera's exhilarating track alongside his run is reminiscent of the end of *The 400 Blows*, where Antoine escapes from imprisonment to a natural expanse.) Moreover, the sculptor takes crushed steel squares from a yard, suggesting that the artist is perhaps a thief (and certainly a deconstructionist). Ben, whose job consists of wrecking walls, calls himself a thief, and we see him steal the credit card of the sculptor's father. But his character has also appropriated iconography from other movies: like Belmondo in *Breathless*, he enters the bar mimicking a gun-toting gangster.

Kaufman's casting is noteworthy. Lou Gilbert—who had appeared in *Viva Zapata* (dir. Elia Kazan, 1952)—was blacklisted; after Fellini saw *Goldstein*, he cast Gilbert in *Juliet of the Spirits* (1965). Since Gilbert also plays the sculptor's wealthy, judgmental father, the film includes an intriguing "doubling" between the mystical hero full of "wonderment" (a resonant term from *The Great Northfield Minnesota Raid*) and a capitalist patriarch. Kaufman pointed out that "the older woman who dances with him is Viola Spolin, who 'wrote the book' on improvisational acting. Del Close, the first leering doctor, was a revered name as a teacher of improv/Second City acting. Severn Darden and Anthony Holland were legends in their own time. And Nelson Algren is the author of *Man with the Golden Arm* and *Walk on the Wild Side*."

Algren, who was a friend of both Kaufman and Simone de Beauvoir, matter-of-factly tells the sculptor a story about a baseball player while the camera tracks along his books and photos of nude women. Also visible is a helmet with a swastika, which makes one wonder if there is a Holocaust inference in the scene of Goldstein being chased into "the smoke house" (which is what the sculptor calls the sausage factory): after being hung from a meathook, the old man is locked in the smoke house and the "cook" dial is turned on. As Columbia student Yaron Lemelbaum proposed in a class discussion, the Jew is pursued there for his otherness. Chicago itself seems like a human factory, with assembly lines, ludicrous police officers, and mechanical female dancers. When Ben seems to be selling the sculptor's creations in an art gallery, he says, "The technical going to the primal"—which is also a theme of the film. Even the shots of sculpture at the beginning dwarf the individuals beside them.

On the occasion of the film's DVD release, Noel Murray noted that "*Goldstein* is fascinating as a cultural document, both for the way it slots between John Cassavetes and the early films of Brian De Palma on the American independent-film timeline, and for the way it captures Chicago's mid-60s art and folk scenes." For the director, the greatest validation came in the form of his French New Wave inspiration: at the first screening of *Goldstein* in Chicago, Kaufman recalled, "[W]ho

Lou Gilbert in *Goldstein*. Courtesy of Walrus and Associates.

should walk in but François Truffaut. He was in town visiting Alexandra Stewart, who had a relationship with him and was shooting *Mickey One* for Arthur Penn. Right in the middle of the screening, Truffaut leaped to his feet and started applauding" (qtd. in Cowie 137).

Many of the actors from *Goldstein* return in *Frank's Greatest Adventure*, shot in 1965 and released in 1967; however, the star of Kaufman's second feature is Jon Voight, a few years before *Midnight Cowboy*. "I had seen him in an off-Broadway production of Arthur Miller's *View from the Bridge*," Kaufman wrote in a letter of March 1, 2005. "The role of Eddie Carbone was played on alternate nights by Richard Castellano (later of *The Godfather*) and Robert Duvall. Dustin Hoffman was the stage manager of the production, still an unknown." The film, also known as *Fearless Frank,* plays with prototypes from comic strips as well as fables (predating Mel Brooks's *Young Frankenstein* [1974] as well as the Batman film adaptations). On the one hand, it can be seen as a sophomoric comic-book tale about a country bumpkin, Frank (Voight), who comes to the big city of Chicago, is killed by mobsters, found by a doctor, and resurrected (in a Frankenstein parallel) as a super hero who can fly in pursuit of evil. But in the light of Kaufman's subsequent development as a filmmaker, its treatment of doubling, surveillance, and manipulation—audaciously blending sources as well as tones—merits analysis. The cinematographer was Bill Butler, who would go on to shoot *The Conversation* (dir. Francis Ford Coppola, 1974), *Jaws* (dir. Steven Spielberg, 1975), and *One Flew over the Cuckoo's Nest* (dir. Milos Forman, 1975).

After Frank is smitten with the caricature Plethora (Monique van Vooren)—a prisoner of the "Boss" (Lou Gilbert)—the self-conscious tone is set by comic-book titles in panels, gleeful music (again by Meyer Kupferman), and the voiceover of "the storyteller." But the Boss's henchmen, "Cat" (Ben Carruthers) and "Rat" (David Steinberg), like the trapped lass with an amulet, suggest a fairy-tale or fable source as well. Plethora seems to have emerged from Fellini's *La Dolce Vita* (1960)—especially when she appears in a fountain à la Anita Ekberg—and the

Jon Voight flying above Chicago in *Fearless Frank*. Courtesy of Walrus and Associates.

circus music also smacks of Fellini's playfulness.[2] Her performance of two songs contributes to Kaufman's almost Brechtian distancing.

"The Good Doctor" (Severn Darden) resurrects the corpse in his lab-mansion—creating a new Frank who will be virtuous—helped by his loyal butler Alfred (Anthony Holland). He inserts into Frank's brain a receiver and dictates orders from a microphone during Frank's dreams. This is perhaps Kaufman's first exploration of being taken over, culminating in *Invasion of the Body Snatchers* and *Twisted.* Also in the house is his bored daughter Lois (Joan Darling): like Plethora, she is trapped in the castle and drawn to Frank. The doctor displays his "evil finder"—a screen framing an evil act that Frank must combat (predating the more sophisticated screens of Spielberg's *Minority Report* in 2002). The budding super hero manages to stop Rat's museum theft, Cat's jewel robbery, and the racetrack crimes of "Needles" (Nelson Algren). But the doctor's "evil" brother Claude (also Darden)—who, like his parrot Werner, has a German accent—works with the Boss to create a "Fake Frank," a double that they can control. This Voight figure includes stitches on the bottom left of his face, continuing on to his shiny metallic grey jacket! Because the first impression on Fake Frank is Plethora's kiss, he ironically becomes an agent of good, while the first Frank succumbs to pride, turning against the doctor who created him. During the showdown between the two Frank creations at an abandoned roller coaster, Fake Frank falls. When the doctor dies of a heart attack, the first Frank assumes his voice. In a Freudian reading, the patriarchal doctor has given life to Frank, treating him like a son. His creation is responsible for the death of the "father" and then becomes a version of him. After Frank wreaks havoc in a bar—even socking a woman (Rose Kaufman) who calls him Ralph—he jumps to his death. It is Fake Frank who ends up in a cell for the real Frank's crime. The voiceover says that he passes into legend as we see a dream scene of him in a boat with Lois and Plethora, rowed by Alfred. Like Goldstein, Frank disappears after having been "reborn" into a world that he views with childlike innocence; only his clothes remain, and they are then taken by the wind.

Frank's Greatest Adventure begins with the voiceover line, "Crime is everywhere." The narrator (Ken Nordine) is actually part of the tale, as we hear, "Oh, that's me!" when he appears. Although he disappears for most of the narrative, he returns at the end, addressing the camera from prison (presumably the place from which he has been composing and narrating his tale). Like the storyteller who often opens Kaufman's films, he is accompanied by a winking eye: here, we see Voight behind twigs (as in *Goldstein*), and we then look through Cat's binoculars in a circular point-of-view shot at Plethora. The self-consciousness is enhanced by the use of zoom (suggesting surveillance) as well as iris shots, and by Rat running backwards through the streets. Reflections abound as Cat robs jewels. And when the doctor listens in on Frank's dreams, a circular mirror in Frank's room literalizes the doubling that will become central to the film. The two images of Frank are balanced by the two images of Severn Darden as "the Good Doctor" and the "evil" Claude, each creating a hero to control. (Frank even bleeds from the place where Fake Frank has stitches.) But, like the legendary Golem, the creation can turn against him.

There is a mock-heroic tone, as Kaufman juggles references from "Lil Abner" to Fritz Lang's *Metropolis* (1927), from *Pygmalion* to Claude's Nazi associations. He acknowledged not only that George Bernard Shaw's *Pygmalion* was a model but that one of his favorite scenes is the parody of *My Fair Lady,* where—instead of "The Rain in Spain"—Voight and Darden develop "'Right Nice Ice Cream' onto a properly British level that reveals precisely how dumb everything can get on the road to supposed wisdom." Vivid images prepare for Kaufman's future films: when smoke freezes nightclub spectators during Plethora's song as the gang steals their jewelry, the zombie look on their faces foreshadows the controlled personalities of *Invasion of the Body Snatchers.* Moreover, images of a mouse running around a dish suggest conditioning—the kind of scientific control that destroys impulse and idiosyncrasy. On the contrary, Frank's yearning for freedom is what makes him human.[3] As Kaufman recalled, "The true Frank comes to mirror the soulless world of his mentor, the Good Doctor, man of science, standard bearer of morality, etc. While the False Frank—a truer Frankenstein sewn-together construct—comes to 'grow a soul' under the tutelage of the daffy brother Claude. In the end, a strange form of comic book 'Good' triumphs, and a film that begins 'stupidly' (with Frank as Sgt. York(?) ends absurdly; but hopefully those who were nurtured on comic books might see how this was somehow about the American dream, particularly during the early years of the Vietnam War. I'm never sure how Good and Evil cross paths, but this was a way I saw (way, way back then) to explore a possible trail through the wilderness . . . and have some fun at the same time."

Fearless Frank includes the first example of a "mentor" relationship, a leitmotif throughout Kaufman's cinema. If the filmmaker himself had mentors such as Henry Miller, we can see Sam Shepard's Yeager in *The Right Stuff,* Sean Connery's Connor in *Rising Sun,* and Geoffrey Rush's Marquis de Sade in *Quills* as parent or teacher figures who help others evolve. But, as Kaufman acknowledged after a conversation with someone who had just seen *The Great Northfield Minnesota Raid* and asked him about the "mentoring" that Jesse James gives to the young Bob Younger, "To be sure, all of his advice is pretty wicked, but so is the Good Doctor's as he mentors 'Frank.'" What is a child to do when a parent proves to be wrong or untrustworthy? Separate and find one's own identity? Appropriately enough, the child or student can be related to the film adapter: one who transforms a book into a motion picture must deal with the source text by balancing fidelity and freedom. Kaufman's "mentor" concern suggests the opposite of "fascist" or manipulative filmmaking: especially when he uses self-conscious devices, his movies partake of an open dialogue with the original novel and with the viewer.

Sexual and Artistic Freedom

The Unbearable Lightness of Being

Three of Kaufman's greatest films center on men who are lucid, sexually promiscuous, and politically subversive because they embody freedom and/or imagination. Moreover, *The Unbearable Lightness of Being* (1987), *Henry and June* (1990), and *Quills* (2000) feature triangular love stories whose erotic energy is evenly diffused among their characters. Close analysis reveals the director's visually poetic shaping and sharpening of literary source material.

Not every great motion picture continues to yield new aspects of stylistic enchantment and thematic depth after a dozen viewings, but *The Unbearable Lightness of Being* is certainly one of them. Despite its approximately three-hour length, not a single frame is gratuitous. Every moment contributes to a vision that comprehends political history (and its representation), perception (and its limitations), personal freedom (and its price), as well as cinematic storytelling. Its source is Milan Kundera's seemingly unadaptable novel of 1984, filled with philosophical asides about eroticism and mortality. Kaufman cowrote the screenplay with Jean-Claude Carrière (Luis Buñuel's accomplice, whose script collaborations include Volker Schlondorff's *The Tin Drum*, Daniel Vigne's *The Return of Martin Guerre*, and Milos Forman's *Valmont* and *Goya's Ghosts*). Indeed, Kaufman recalled in 2002 that Forman—who had been a student of Kundera's at the Czech film school—offered him the project: "Milos had been approached before me to do Kundera's book by a producer (before Saul Zaentz got involved). But with two boys living in Prague, it was too risky a project for him to do. He knew how much I admired the book and called me to see if I was interested." Unable to film this testament to freedom in Communist Czechoslovakia, he shot in Lyons, France, using the Czech filmmaker Jan Nemec—who lived through the late 1960s in Prague—as an advisor. (Nemec has a cameo as the photographer who is accused by the interrogator during the Soviet-invasion sequence.) Together with the cinematographer Sven Nykvist (best known for Ingmar Bergman's films), they created a sumptuous visual tale as well as a complex meditation on voyeurism, politics, and morality. Pauline Kael's enthusiastic review in the *New Yorker* proposes succinctly: "Unbearable lightness refers to our recognizing that we go through life only once—it's like going onstage unrehearsed. And, more specifically, it's the suspended state of a person in an occupied country" (Kael, "Take Off," 67).

Set in 1968 Prague, the film begins like an erotic comedy, turns into a political tragedy, and ends in a domestic pastoral. Tomas (Daniel Day-Lewis, before his international success in *My Left Foot* [1989]) is a young surgeon and an irresistible playboy. His most important lover is the uninhibited artist Sabina (Lena Olin), but he is drawn to the waitress Tereza (Juliette Binoche, long before *The English Patient* [1996]) during his visit to her spa town to perform an operation. When she shows up on his Prague doorstep, he flirts with her almost amusedly, while she responds with violent passion. For the first time, he lets a woman stay overnight in his bed, and she later gets him to marry her. Despite Tereza's touching vulnerability, peasant-like charm, and love for Tomas, he continues to philander, especially with Sabina (who helps Tereza get work as a photographer).

With her camera, Tereza captures the Soviet invasion that suddenly crushes the Prague Spring. Under political pressure, she and Tomas leave for Geneva. Sabina is also in Geneva, where she has embarked on an affair with Franz (Derek de Lint), a handsome (and married) professor. Tereza visits Sabina, ostensibly because she needs shots of female nudes to get photographic work. After this sequence of playful eroticism charged with darker emotions, Tereza leaves Tomas and returns to Prague, supposedly because she feels too dependent on him: "I'm weak. I'm going back to the country of the weak," she admits. But he follows her, fully aware they will have to remain in Prague. Because he once wrote an article criticizing the government, he can't get his job back without signing a retraction. He refuses, even after the Interior Ministry official (Daniel Olbrychski) coaxes him to do so. If Tomas initially seemed like an amoral Don Juan, he becomes a political hero when he refuses to sign.

Tereza finally decides to even out the adulterous score of the marriage and goes to the apartment of an engineer (Stellan Skarsgard) who protected and flirted with her at the bar where she works. Later realizing from a former ambassador who is now a janitor (Erland Josephson) that she might have been set up for blackmail, she makes Tomas move with her to the countryside, where they stay with the jolly Pavel (Pavel Landovsky). Life seems blissful, but Sabina—now in California—receives a letter saying that they died in a car crash. We cut back to Tomas and Tereza alive, on the road, fading to white before the accident.

Using the music of the Czech composer Leos Janacek—suggested by Kundera—Kaufman provides a structure that could be called musical: we move from "andante" to "adagio," from light—visually and thematically—to dark, and from quick cuts to longer takes (as is true of Truffaut's *Jules and Jim* [1962], another splendid adaptation that traces the attempt of characters to love more than one person at one time). The care with which Kaufman constructed each scene merits our close analysis, with attention to cinematic details anchoring understanding of his methods and insights. As Columbia student T'sera Mingst-Belcher wrote in an unpublished paper, "*The Unbearable Lightness of Being,* as cinema, is at somewhat of a disadvantage to the novel because each frame is more fleeting than the page. Whereas a book is like the building up of grains of sand in a jar, a film is more like watching them blow past in the wind.

To obtain the same effect as a novel, each frame of a film must contain a great deal more than a paragraph or a page. It must take the meaning of an entire scene or pregnant occurrence in the novel and render it concretely in the mise-en-scène" (3). How does *The Unbearable Lightness of Being* succeed in this goal?

The film's action is preceded by the sound of a woman's laughter behind a closed door—as well as cooing doves—and a title card: "In Prague, in 1968, there lived a young doctor named Tomas." Reminiscent of silent movies, the title introduces not only the protagonist but his charged place and time in terms of sexual as well as political revolution. In addition, its fairy-tale tone creates comic self-consciousness, heightened by the sense of a line translated into English from a foreign language. By having us "read" the screen, Kaufman thus begins not simply with an acknowledgment of a literary source but a refusal of voice. This immediately separates his motion picture from Kundera's novel, which opens with the vocal speculation of the first-person narrator. Unlike the book's first paragraph—"The idea of eternal return is a mysterious one, and Nietzsche has often perplexed other philosophers with it: to think that everything recurs as we once experienced it, and that the recurrence itself recurs ad infinitum! What does this mad myth signify?" (Kundera 3)—the film playfully celebrates the visual.

The opening sequence consists of five scenes, beginning with a literal spark: a beautiful nurse strikes a match to light a cigarette, virtually igniting the film. "Take off your clothes," Tomas says to her from under a towel. "What?" "Take off your clothes," he repeats, now visible. As she complies, the camera pulls back to reveal that they are watched by a patient lying on the other side of the window, as well as a doctor standing next to him. Since our own voyeurism is shared by secondary characters, Kaufman invites our gaze at the same time that he makes us aware of internal frames. The juxtaposition of eroticism and self-consciousness continues in the second scene, which is introduced by the title, "But the woman who understood him best was Sabina." She and Tomas lie on her bed, his head covering her naked breast, her bowler hat masking part of her face. As they move more fully into view, their lovemaking includes a vividly visual dimension: the oval mirror next to the bed not only permits Tomas and Sabina to look at themselves; it opens up another plane for the audience as well, reflecting itself into the heart of the frame. Kaufman thus invokes "eternal return" in a cinematic manner, the image repeating itself infinitely. (The bowler hat itself suggests eternal return, reappearing at key moments; when Tomas later likens it to Sabina's essence, she traces its history from "a long, long time ago.") Columbia student Juliet Berman wrote, "[T]he fragmentation of reality that the mirror establishes has a phenomenological effect. The viewer becomes instantly aware of his or her own process of visual perception. Like a cubist painting, the screen is not a window into another world, but a flattened canvas, an image of reality rather than reality itself" (1).

If Kundera begins his novel with the concept of eternal return, Kaufman visually translates it into reflected images and repeated motifs. There is great coherence in his literal as well as figurative mirrors. While the most striking emblem of eternal return is the shot of Tomas and Sabina making love between two mirrors—reflected infinitely into the depth of the screen—other circular images express the theme as well. For example, Tomas rides a merry-go-round in Geneva; and when he visits Sabina there, their initial hesitancy is overcome when she places the bowler hat on her head: they twirl around passionately until the hat falls off, spiraling like a top as it falls by the mirror.

The credits unfold in the third scene, as Tomas drives from Prague to a spa town. After a close-up of his eyes behind dark glasses, he removes them and we see his gaze. Kaufman continues the motif of interrupted sight: we move from Kundera's abstraction to visual obstruction—whether a towel, a hat, a head, or sunglasses—followed by revelation. The director teases the audience just enough to make us aware of something withheld, and then finally granted. The fourth scene juxtaposes the surgical operation Tomas performs, with a band performing a vigorous march song outside. A close-up of the bulbous cheeks of a bassoonist rhymes with the close-up of a black balloon on the operating table. Tomas hums the tune as he deftly handles his surgical instruments. Moreover, Kaufman's two-shot of Tomas and a female nurse beside him adds an enigmatic note: behind the surgical mask, her breath is visibly accelerating, as if she were excited by his proximity. Similarly, he is ogled appreciatively by two young women after completing the operation. Kaufman's emphasis on voyeurism and seduction is not only faithful to Kundera's themes but celebratory of his visual medium.

In the fifth scene, Tomas's attention is diverted from a chess match of six men in the swimming pool to the graceful dive of Tereza: innocent of his gaze, she jumps, swims the length of the pool, and steps out. That Tomas is smitten is visibly suggested by the black knight toppling over the chessboard, followed by a quick cut to Tomas. When she changes behind a curtain, she takes off her clothes without Tomas even asking. He sees Tereza as we have seen him, behind things and then revealed. He pursues her through foggy corridors of steam, as fire and water blend in Kaufman's elemental vision. Reminiscent of Fellini's *8½* (1963), the locale is voluptuously dreamlike, including offscreen moans of those being massaged.[4] Tereza enters the café where she is a waitress as Tomas sits down. Her eyes discover him, and he mouths the word "cognac." We see but do not hear Tomas, as opposed to his first words in the film, "Take off your clothes": the nurse hears him but does not see his face. As in the opening scene, his game of seduction invites a repetition: Tereza has not understood, so he repeats, "cognac."

While it would be enlightening to proceed with close analysis of every scene that comprises the rest of *The Unbearable Lightness of Being*, let us return economically to a few of the key ways in which Kaufman tells and illuminates the story. "Cognac" provides a starting point to appreciate repetition of images as well as motifs. Cognac is also what Tomas orders from a more assured—and therefore less compelling—waitress in Switzerland after his wife's abrupt departure, inviting us to remember (even if subliminally) his first interchange with Tereza. And an inebriated youth at the bar where she works gets Tereza intro trouble in the latter part of the film by demanding cognac too. While one can simply conclude that cognac is often ordered in Europe, its repetition adds structural coherence and resonance. Similarly, two train rides in *The Unbearable Lightness of Being* can be contrasted: that of Sabina and Franz is erotic, while Tereza's return to Prague is bleak. Tomas does not take trains, however: he drives to Tereza twice—unwittingly at the beginning, and then again, knowingly, from Geneva to Czechoslovakia. Our final view of him is behind the wheel as well.

Some of the repetitions are simple, like the phrase, "Take off your clothes," which Tomas says four times. Similarly, the swans around the solitary Tomas in the Swiss lake can be connected to those of the Prague lake where Tereza seems to see a bench floating: this image is reminiscent of Tomas and Tereza seated on the bench during their first "date" before he leaves her spa town. Or if Tomas uses the line, "I'm a doctor," to get Tereza to remove her clothes in his apartment, Sabina says, "I'm an artist," toward the same goal when she photographs Tereza. The Czech nurse counts "one, two, three" in the first scene before showing Tomas her breasts; the film's editing creates "one, two, three" with freeze frames of a soldier aiming a gun at Tereza's lens.

But the doubling enacted via mirrors and other reflecting surfaces is complex. During a frankly erotic scene, Sabina straddles the mirror on the floor and asks Tomas, "what are you looking at?" He replies, "Your eyes"—arguably the most sexually vibrant part of a human being. (Sabina's question is echoed by the engineer when Tereza visits his apartment.) Mirrors literalize that, for some, to be seen is to exist—reflection as confirmation of one's substance. But mirrors also juxtapose with the "real" individual an image of weightlessness: does being seen make one less light? As T'sera Mingst-Belcher wrote in an unpublished paper, "Mirrors especially are the perfect visual tools for rendering side-by-side the idea of lightness and weight, or, alternatively, form and substance, ideal and actual, or fleeting and permanent" (2). In either case, the film's mirrors heighten both the exhibitionist nature of Tomas with Sabina and the audience's awareness of our privileged status as spectators. They

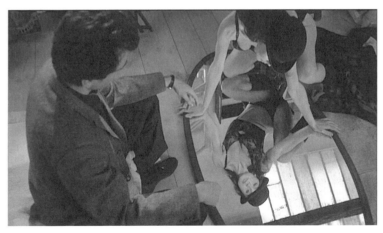

Sabina (Lena Olin) and Tomas (Daniel Day-Lewis) in *The Unbearable Lightness of Being*. Digital frame enlargement.

also function, as Juliet Berman wrote in a student paper, "like a lens, translating rather than imitating, filtering rather than merely reflecting. The reflection is like the film itself, a version of reality without any of its indexical physicality. The viewer and the object are once removed, separated by an intermediary agent" (3–4). (Tereza is framed—literally, figuratively, and unwittingly—when the janitor warns her that the engineer might be an agent of the state: she does not see her own reflection in the bar's mirror.)

Kaufman's voyeurism is, after all, quite benign. For example, Sabina and Franz make love in a train compartment whose sole other passenger pretends to be sleeping: as the man puts on his glasses before seeming to close his eyes, he becomes an audience surrogate, almost inviting us to peep along with him. (The man is played by Pierre Guffroy, the film's production designer.) This sequence illustrates a comment made by Columbia student Jo Budzilowicz about spectator identification: most women might ask, "Who would you rather be, Tereza or Sabina?" while most men would ask, "Whom would you rather be with?" Kaufman's erotic ocularity applies as much to the viewers as the characters, given his predilection for shooting Tomas, Tereza, and Sabina not via abstracted body parts but embodied faces. Is the sensuality not more intense when the entire person is visible?

The director created striking visual equivalents for Kundera's words. Sabina straddling the mirror conveys the lightness of being, especially when Tomas lifts her. Later, in Geneva, she creates a sculpture from mirror shards—in the form of a female body, with Sabina's signature bowler hat on top—which shares the frame with her undressing. Reflecting the air openly, her art is a virtual embodiment of lightness. (Sabina's pieces were actually created by Irena Dedicova, upon whom Kundera based the character of Sabina.) Tereza's lightness, however, is expressed by immersion in swimming pools, beginning with our first glance of her (which coincides with Tomas's). Her second scene in a pool is more troublesome: the point of view alternates between objective (we see Tereza) and subjective (we see through her eyes as a group of women in bathing suits becomes a hallucination of Tomas giving orders to the now-naked females). The third pool scene follows her sexual encounter with the engineer: in slow motion, as if weightless, she floats. In the context of lightness, how appropriate that—when Tomas is reduced to menial work after refusing to sign the retraction—he becomes a window washer, often suspended on high floors.

Kaufman also brilliantly utilizes doorways to suggest the uncertainty of male-female relationships, beginning with Tomas's feigned casualness when Tereza arrives on his doorstep. Subsequently, her rage at his infidelity—which leads her to run out at night—is subsumed by the Soviet invasion of Prague as both stand, frozen at their building's entrance, before the tanks. A scene of personal betrayal thus becomes political and unifies the couple against the occupiers. When Tomas first visits Sabina in Switzerland, they do not immediately jump into one another's arms; their game of withholding is played at the door until he glimpses her bowler hat, which incites their joyous clasping. Likewise, his return to Prague is initially confined to the doorway: this time, it is Tereza who opens the door, where the dog welcomes him before the lovers' tentative reacquaintance in the entryway (so different from the chill of the novel [34 and 76]). It is therefore especially touching when, in the penultimate sequence at the inn, Tomas brings Teresa up to room 6—carrying her (rather light) weight on his feet—invoking the room 6 in which he stayed at the spa but which she did not get to enter on the day they met. The camera lingers as they pass the door's threshold, until we are shut out of the room (not unlike how Tomas was dismissed by Tereza from her photographic darkroom).

Obstruction and revelation are prominent themes as well as devices throughout *The Unbearable Lightness of Being.* In addition to the opening images described above, we are made aware of the limitations of our perception by curtains in at least three scenes: Tereza's silhouette as she dries off after the first swim; Sabina pulling the curtain when Tereza is photographing her nude; the engineer's attempt to convince Tereza that nobody is hiding behind curtains in his apartment by pulling them open and shut. (In the novel, there is no suggestion of someone peering, which fuels Tereza's sense of danger in the film.) If the engineer is first introduced in the bar behind a newspaper, the interrogator of Tereza is also behind a photo before it is lowered to reveal his face; and the soapy window Tomas is cleaning finally reveals Prague when he wipes it. Even the dancing couples at the inn of the penultimate sequence prevent Tomas and Tereza from seeing each other, and then keep the audience from a clear view of the loving duo.

A reflected and reflective Tomas (Daniel
Day-Lewis) admires the bowler hat of
Sabina (Lena Olin) in *The Unbearable Lightness
of Being*. Digital frame enlargement.

Kaufman's reminders of our voyeurism feed into his larger theme
of seeing, both sanctioned and forbidden. How much are we allowed
to see? This question applies to the filmmakers, given that we are often
not permitted to see parts of the frame until a moment of revelation. It
certainly applies to the totalitarian state, which tries to keep its citizens in
the dark (and uses surveillance—a de-eroticized form of voyeurism—to
maintain control). And, most intriguingly, how much are we allowed to
see by our own selves? The incorporation of *Oedipus Rex*—the story of
a man who is metaphorically blind and then takes out his own eyes when
he cannot bear the sight of his crimes—enriches this aspect of the film.
Tereza's nightmares demonstrate involuntary voyeurism, a projection
of what she can't allow herself to see otherwise.

Kaufman's constant visual engagement of the audience relies partly
on the characters' intensely physical means of communication. For instance, the clasping of hands is a potent expression of deep connection
throughout the film. When Tomas awakens from his first night with
Tereza, he finds that she still grips his hand in her sleep: to extricate
himself, he replaces his hand with a copy of *Oedipus Rex* (the very book
whose presence reassures her in the engineer's apartment). Given that
Sophocles's text was under her fingertips, the nightmare she describes

to Tomas of sticking needles into her fingers is painfully apt. When Sabina photographs Tereza lying face down on the couch, she holds her hand, clasping it behind Tereza's back. The last rendezvous of Tomas and Sabina in the Swiss hotel is emotionally deepened by their entwined hands. How eloquent then is Tereza's clenched—and empty—fist when the engineer seduces her.

The next shot is of Tereza floating in slow motion—as limp as she was during sex—in a swimming pool, whose surface is green like the engineer's sweater. This is a departure from the novel, in which Tereza is described as "naked, on a toilet, with a sudden desire to void her bowels" (156). Here we see how Kaufman visually associates her with an elemental lightness, enriched by the recurrence of a lyrical melody on piano. This music is first heard during her introductory dive into the swimming pool. It returns in scenes of Tereza—occasionally in counterpoint with Tomas's cello-based melody—and mainly in a major key. However, it sometimes switches to a minor key, conveying a mournful or ominous tone, appropriate to life after Soviet occupation. A fine example is the scene at the doorway when Tomas follows Tereza to the underworld of Prague: unlike the novel, which describes them as if "standing on a snow-covered plain, shivering with cold" (77), the film presents their tantalizing sudden physical proximity. It begins with her melody in a major key, shifts to the minor key, and returns to the major key when they finally kiss.

Kaufman utilizes musical repetition as deftly as visual rhyming. If the band in the spa town plays a Czech anthem after Tomas operates, the return of the song during the Soviet invasion means resistance. If the Russian anthem is turned into a rock song for dancing in the nightclub sequence at the Golem—thereby angering the Russian authorities, who walk out—it provides a dour sound bridge from Tomas washing windows to Tereza working as a barmaid in a dank Prague café. The atonal, screeching strings that we hear while Tereza is interrogated and when she returns to Prague recur after the janitor/ambassador warns her that she might have been set up for blackmail. The nondiegetic string moments could be called the film's "weakness theme."

These musical echoes are part of a larger understanding on the filmmakers' part, namely that the "book has a musical form," as Kaufman puts it. Like *The Right Stuff*, this cinematic translation of *The Unbearable*

Lightness of Being is anchored in a "theme and variations" approach, whether its focus is perception, occupation, or freedom. If Kundera writes that lives are composed like music (52), Kaufman's characters live with and often via music. Tereza's first action upon entering the bar following her swim is to turn on the radio, whose romantic melody continues during Tomas's flirtation with her. The sound track is an integral narrative element, as Leos Janacek's melodies replace Kundera's first-person rumination. (Kundera's father studied with Janacek, who is mentioned in the book [97].)

The changes from the novel are numerous, radical, and cinematically vibrant. Kundera's Tomas is older and has a son from a previous marriage; his Sabina is divorced. His Tereza lives with her mother, whom we see and hear, and his Franz is a major character in a kind of quartet. The ellipses of Kaufman and Carrière's script streamline the book into a triangular love story among equals. For example, Kundera's Tomas rents a room for Tereza when she shows up in Prague. Their initial lovemaking has no dialogue: "Ten days later she paid him a visit. They made love the day she arrived. That night she came down with a fever and stayed a whole week in his flat with the flu" (6). Kaufman turns this into a comic medical examination–cum-seduction, accompanied by quick, lively strings. He transforms inner monologues into intensely physical scenes, while interweaving aspects of voyeurism or perception in general. For instance, Kundera's Tereza tells Tomas of her nightmare, in which she is one of twenty naked females at an indoor swimming pool, where Tomas shoots women with a gun (18). The author describes the dream again later, emphasizing Tereza's nakedness (57). In the film, she is swimming (wearing a bathing suit) and suddenly sees Tomas directing naked women in the pool. Tereza is now compelled to watch, an unwilling voyeur. (This is also the case in her description to Tomas of her nightmare, where she is forced to look at his lovemaking with Sabina.)

Kaufman replaces the "I" of Kundera's text with the "eye" of cinematic storytelling—an appropriate substitution for a work that alludes more than once to Sophocles's *Oedipus Rex*. And it is eye contact that brings Tomas together with Tereza when he visits her town. Here is how the novel presents their initial contact: "He had first met Tereza about three weeks earlier in a small Czech town. They had spent scarcely an hour together. She had accompanied him to the station and waited with him until he boarded the train" (6). Subsequently, Kundera muses on destiny: "The town had several hotels, but Tomas happened to be given a room in the one where Tereza was employed. He happened to have had enough free time before his train left to stop at the hotel restaurant. Tereza happened to be on duty, and happened to be serving Tomas's table. It had taken six chance happenings to push Tomas towards Tereza, as if he had little inclination to go to her on his own" (35).

The film turns the locale into a spa town, redolent of steam baths, where an offscreen massage evokes sounds indistinguishable from sexual moans. Tomas's gaze follows her underwater glide through the pool and then to the curtain behind which she dries herself with a towel. Watching the silhouette of her naked body, Tomas then follows her—through the mist-filled corridors of the spa—into the café where she works. He sees Tereza as we have seen him in previous scenes: if his face was behind a towel, then a surgical mask, she is temporarily obscured by water, then a curtain, and finally steam. In the café, her own eyes (in a subjective shot) find Tomas, who pretends to be reading. By the time they finally speak, the atmosphere is charged with the simmering sexual attraction between Tomas and Tereza. In a departure from the novel, their eyes suggest desire—or free will—rather than chance.

Similarly, Kundera describes Tereza on the day she meets Tomas in terms of heaviness: "[H]er body sagged under the weight of the beers on the tray, and her soul lay somewhere at the level of the stomach or pancreas" (47). The film transforms this into Tereza's supremely light swim from one side of the pool to the other, under Tomas's suddenly attentive gaze. Indeed, the first twenty minutes of the film zip by with an economy that is appropriate to the cinematic medium: one could say that Kaufman's ellipses are "econocomical," rendering humorous Tomas's relationship to women and work (capturing the exhilaration of the heady Prague Spring). Later, Kaufman's streamlining of the book is deft and dramatically riveting. After returning to Prague, Tomas is suddenly a clinic doctor; then, after refusing to sign the retraction, he is suddenly washing windows. This suggests the abrupt and absurd shifts that characterize life under Communism. If Kundera's Tereza photographs Russian soldiers over seven days, the film compresses the Soviet invasion into a terse six minutes. And if we learn in the novel that she has been with Tomas for seven years before she decides to leave Switzerland for

Prague (76), the film makes it seem like less time has passed. Indeed, her decision to return seems unrelated in the book to her photographic session with Sabina, while the film's juxtaposition of the sensual photos and her brusque departure suggests that Tereza cannot bear to remain in the same city as Sabina.

Kundera's sketchy account of Tereza photographing Sabina nude (65) is merely a point of departure for the film's memorable sequence of—and about—a layered voyeurism. Whereas the repeated word in the book is "strip," Sabina says to Tereza the less vulgar "look at me" more than once. There are numerous layers in the looks exchanged between the two women, as well as those of the spectator. (The camera placement enables the privileged viewer to see each of their faces even when Sabina and Tereza are positioned behind one another.) Besides the obvious aspects of curiosity, desire, and jealousy, guilt plays a role: Sabina lies to Tereza that she has not seen Tomas. In addition to Kundera's description of the camera serving "Tereza as both a mechanical eye through which to observe Tomas's mistress and a veil by which to conceal her face from her" (65) as well as "a weapon" (66), the lens is an excuse, a shield, and a means of control. Moreover, Sabina's window-filled apartment allows the weather itself to express the turbulence of the characters' feelings, like the rain with Tereza's tears (hidden by the camera), or the storm after Sabina removes her robe. The presence of mirrors heightens our awareness of the act of looking and the sense that we are in Sabina's domain, where Tomas's presence has been inscribed. If Tereza's darkroom mirror is square and professional (the real way to dry photos), Sabina's is oval and sexual. As Sabina undresses, we see her sculpture, a reflecting surface of a female shape, topped by her bowler hat (Tomas is quite present in his absence). Later, her shards multiply Tereza—reluctant, giggling, and naked—creating comical complicity within and beyond the frame. Nevertheless, there is a noteworthy ellipsis before the sequence ends on the two nude women laughing in front of the fireplace: Did they kiss each other since we last saw them? Or more? An uncomprehending Franz makes his entrance; while he doesn't know what has transpired, we have been privileged spectators . . . but only up to a point. There is a tension between the privileges and limitations that Kaufman bestows upon us as spectators. Isn't he playing an elaborate game of seduction with the viewer by not showing us what transpired between Tereza and Sabina? He lets us glimpse an intimate moment and then abruptly cuts, leaving us wanting more.

In the novel, Franz is absent from the scene, which simply ends with the two women laughing and getting dressed, followed by Kundera's account of Tereza's photos of the Russian invasion. Again, his brief summary of her picture taking (67) is like a negative that is masterfully developed by the film into a richly textured portrait. Walter Murch seamlessly cross-cut newsreel footage with new shots of Tomas and Tereza that were purposely scratched or desaturated to appear like "found" footage. Even Jan Nemec—who originally shot much of the invasion footage—is seen shooting from the balcony, purposely made grainy, as if he, too, were in his own past. (Tereza's photographs are all stills of real footage taken in 1968.) We feel the chaos within the frame, as well as the precise control of its presentation. The film moves in and out of color; the eyes of a statue are blindfolded; the crowd breathlessly repeats the name of its revered leader, "Dubcek, Dubcek"; and sudden freeze frames are like the holding of one's breath.

Photography itself, capturing a fleeting moment forever, can be likened to eternal return, especially because Kaufman uses the freeze

Teresa (Juliette Binoche) and Tomas (Daniel Day-Lewis) during the Soviet invasion of Prague in *The Unbearable Lightness of Being.* Digital frame enlargement.

frames to heighten politically charged moments during the Soviet-invasion sequence. When Tereza photographs a soldier who is confronting her with a gun, the three increasingly menacing freeze frames of his stern face demonstrate that she will not submit, that she is indeed "shooting" him—repeatedly—with her own weapon. However, the third time that his gun waving is frozen into her photograph turns out to be a troubling segue into the following sequence of interrogation. As the photo of the soldier is lowered, another face is revealed: the interrogator (Laszlo Szabo) is using the photographs as evidence—a means of identifying those in the crowd. The solidity of these frames enables those in power to arrest the resisters. Her photographs embody the contrast between lightness and weight: when used as evidence, they assume solidity; but in the context of the film itself, the images appear momentarily before vanishing. Similarly, the freeze frame punctuates the rapid movement of projected celluloid, making us aware of the duality of the cinematic image.

For the invasion sequence, the script delineates three stages—"The Occupation," "Resistance, Czech Style," and "The Russian Retaliation"—ending with Tereza "shooting" the tank commander with her camera. But it was apparently in postproduction that the brilliant decision was made to repeat the freeze frame three times and to use it as a transition to the subsequent scene of interrogation. The screenplay by Jean-Claude Carrière and Kaufman (whose second draft, dated August 5, 1986, the director graciously made available to me) is instructive in terms of what was planned for the film, what was created afterwards, and what was left out. As one might expect, numerous scenes and lines were later deleted. Many of the minor alterations are in the service of stylistic and thematic coherence, especially with respect to voyeurism. For example, the script has Tomas first seeing Tereza in the pool and then waiting near "the changing room"; the film adds a huge mirror behind Tomas and has her changing as a tantalizing silhouette through a curtain. Kaufman also deleted subsequent scenes: Tomas scribbling his address on a piece of paper for Tereza as he drives away, or her arrival at Prague's railway station, struggling with an enormous suitcase and then lugging it to a crowded café. In the film, she simply appears on his doorstep, as if she divined his whereabouts.[5] In the script, she arrives at night, awakening Tomas; in the film, it is daytime and he is eating an apple (yes, there will be temptation). The script's sequence ends with a feverish Tereza telling him that she has nowhere to stay and Tomas retrieving her suitcase from the hallway. It cuts to him at the hospital informing the nurse from the opening scene that he can't see her that night, and then to him waking up to find the sleeping Tereza grasping his hand. The film places this "hand" moments earlier, compressing their first romantic interchange into a few hours, while cutting out the other scenes. As Columbia student Chris Wells wrote in an unpublished paper, "By dispensing with labored segues, Kaufman created ambiguous ellipses in the story, narrative gaps that let audience members connect the dots for themselves. . . . In fact, this is one of the filmmaker's main achievements in his adaptation of Kundera's novel: he learned to have more faith in, and respect for, his audience. A perfect illustration of this trust appears on page 45. The script has Tereza play the music that was heard when she first met Tomas—a Beethoven quartet—and identify it as such out loud. In the movie, however, Kaufman simply lets the music play on the sound track. He allows, and trusts, viewers to make the aural association for themselves, to put the pieces of these fractured characters and stories together. In the same way that these characters seek to complete one another, the audience must complete the empty spaces in the narrative" (4–5).

Chunks of dialogue disappeared from script to screen—notably, Tereza confessing to Sabina at the end of their photography session that she is terribly weak, and the chief surgeon predicting that Tomas will work in a provincial clinic because he refused to sign the retraction. Sharp visual details were obviously added later: for instance, Tomas simply pushes away the minister's retraction letter in the script but tosses it into this character's hat in the film. The slight change reminds us of the bowler hat that was a sign of his erotic contract with Sabina—whereas he has no contract with the political authorities. The screenplay introduces the engineer as simply observing Tereza and her accuser at the bar, but the film places him behind a newspaper before he reveals his face, "rhyming" his introduction with that of other initially obstructed characters. As Juliet Berman proposed in an April 2008 class discussion, "By making us active participants in the movie-watching process, he hearkens back to the act of reading, which is more interactive in the sense that we must constantly create meaning from the words on the page. Similarly, instead of letting us passively observe, Kaufman forces us to act as interpreters, 'reading' his film the way we would a novel."

Tomas dismisses a government minister (Daniel Olbrychski) who asks him to sign a retraction in *The Unbearable Lightness of Being*. Digital frame enlargement.

Most significantly, the screenplay includes toward the end a scene of Tomas driving the truck whose brakes malfunction: "We better get these brakes fixed," he says. Similarly, a scene of Tomas driving the same truck when a tire blows out—the truck skids, slides to a stop, and smashes a sign—is deleted. These omissions remove the foreshadowing of their death, rendering it more of a shock.

The last section of *The Unbearable Lightness of Being* is a fascinating departure from the script's blueprint. The original vision of Kaufman and Carrière includes three scenes that the director later deleted: 1) in their room at the inn, Tomas and Tereza talk and dance as the camera moves to the window from which we can see the fatal truck; 2) as on the novel's last page, a moth flutters around a lamp while they kiss; 3) they are on the Prague bridge, with their dog Karenin (whom we know to be dead). Whereas the novel informs us—less than midway through—that Tomas and Tereza died (via a letter from his son to Sabina in Paris [122]), the film places her in the expanse of a California beach, receiving this news toward the end from Pavel's letter. Rather than having to show the crash, the ending is more oblique and lyrical: on the road, sitting close together in the truck, Tereza asks Tomas what he is thinking. He replies, "I'm thinking how happy I am." The return of Tereza's melody accompanies the falling rain, the gentle music soothing what we now know are their last moments. With a fade to white, the film ends with "lightness" in the double sense of illumination and a lack of heaviness. Moreover, prominent in these last shots is the windshield wiper, an instrument of clarity reminiscent of Tomas washing windows. It sounds like a metronome (continuing Kundera's image of lives as musical compositions) and also invokes *The Conformist* (1970), where close-ups of windshield wipers express Berrnardo Bertolucci's similar concern with voyeurism, blindness, and perception.

"I actually shot a few possible endings for the film, not totally satisfied with each after I saw them in the dailies," Kaufman recalled in October 2004.

> The first had Tomas and Tereza dancing with each other in the room at the inn.
>
> It was a difficult shot, with them dancing slowly around and around while the camera circled around them. At the end of the shot the camera moves past them and out the window, looking down on the dark truck standing there waiting to carry them to their doom (as we already know). This would have recalled a shot earlier in the film when Tomas lifted Sabina in Geneva and they joyously circled around and around with the camera ending on her black bowler hat which had fallen off. The second was closer to the book: they were in bed together, and the camera drifted off to a moth circling around the light next to their bed. Third was Tomas and Tereza walking over the Charles Bridge . . . on a foggy night. They are hand in hand, happy, though we already have the information that they have died. Then a sudden bark; and as they turned, Karenin came rushing over the bridge to join them, and the three walked away happily: Unbearable Lightness only in the Hereafter. All shots were interesting, but none of them . . . delivered the emotional impact we needed. In the editing room, I was working through other film we had shot and when I came across that POV shot going down the wooded country road and saw that sudden moment of lightness, I knew. The lines were added in looping sessions.

Seeing Tomas and Tereza again after Sabina receives the letter constitutes another example of eternal return: they are forever alive in the film's loop. The "weight" of their relationship has evolved from a burden to support. When Tomas carries Tereza into room 6, her weight—or lightness—on his feet is bearable to him. She certainly has more "substance" than at the beginning: in this film where a window washer is really a surgeon, or a janitor an ambassador, only Tereza remains a waitress. But the greatest dramatic arc is hers, as she develops from an awkward provincial, to a photographer with political convictions, to a nurturer. Her transformation is more appreciable than in the novel, partly because we see her photos—the contents as well as confident capturing—and partly because of Binoche's nuanced depiction, physically and spiritually. Pauline Kael's review calls attention to how "the young Binoche gives the role a sweet gaucheness and then a red-cheeked desperation—the push and pathos of a Clara Bow or a young Susan Hayward" ("Take Off" 69).

Kael also confesses to having reservations about Kundera's book and then celebrates the film's achievement: "[W]hile watching the movie I began to feel more affection for the novel. . . . Kaufman cuts down on the pastry pensées, and the movie has some of his adventurous spirit. It's a prankish sex comedy that treats modern political events with a delicate—yet almost sly—sense of tragedy. It's touching in sophisticated ways that you don't expect from an American director" (67).

Kundera urged Kaufman to "eliminate" whenever possible, well aware that an adaptation of his novel could not be faithful. On January 5, 1988, the director wrote a letter to the author and his wife, announcing the film's completion:

> Milan, what a strange relationship we have—novelist and director. Where else does something like this exist? You said you shouldn't be on the set watching me film, that it would be like a father watching someone make love to his daughter. And I must admit it was a pleasure. I went off and violated your work . . . but at the same time tried to remain faithful. I fucked it with reverence. Between us there is the makings of a strange religion.
>
> Now we both must wait nervously to see how you respond. I remind you that mysterious things happened once the screenplay encountered actors, locations, camera moves and lighting, montage, and all the joys and sorrows of filming. What you will be seeing is truly a variation rather than an adaptation, a thread pulled from the fabric of the novel, a melodic line developed from your complex themes. It lacks the most interesting character of the novel—the Narrator. It lacks the precise

musical structure as well. But another musical structure might have emerged, found somewhere in motifs repeated, in visuals, and in sound. And the Narrator, like a dybbuk, finds his way (at times) into the mouths of characters; or maybe he's hidden in the persistent Janacek score. Maybe (at times) Janacek speaks for Kundera.

Kaufman enjoyed a degree of freedom that permitted him to shift the focus of the book from a philosophical rumination to a love story. As in his subsequent film, *Henry and June,* the director substitutes an "eye" for an "I," celebrating the visual that takes flight from the verbal.

Henry and June

Henry and June (1990) demonstrates how to cinematically adapt an extremely verbal text with wit as well as eroticism. A "family affair," it was scripted by Kaufman with his wife Rose and produced by their son Peter. The film's roots are not simply in the sensuous journals of Anaïs Nin but in the director's early passion for Henry Miller's writing: when he hitchhiked through Europe, he tried to smuggle *Tropic of Cancer* past customs, hidden in his underwear (Sragow, "Fearless Phil," 13–14). Since *Henry and June* was the first film to receive the NC-17 rating in the United States, it shares with the work of Nin and Miller the distinction of being deemed dangerous. And it is clearly a companion piece to *The Unbearable Lightness of Being,* elaborating on the themes of voyeurism and desire. The cinematography of Philippe Rousselot richly re-creates Paris in the 1930s—a period of liberation comparable to Prague in 1968—anchoring the narrative in the expressive faces of Maria de Medeiros as Anaïs and of Uma Thurman as Henry's wife June.

Anaïs is married to the proper, sweet, and British Hugo (Richard E. Grant), who brings to their home the brash, macho, and entertaining Henry Miller (Fred Ward). Anaïs is swept up in the American writer's world, especially when they read each other's work; however, it is the dusky June to whom she is erotically—and mutually—drawn. On their last night together before June returns to New York—which includes a visit to a lesbian bar—she essentially tells Anaïs to take care of Henry in her absence. It seems that Anaïs is then drawn sexually to Henry because she is identifying with June, wanting to feel what she feels. Subsequently, after becoming Henry's mistress, is Anaïs then drawn to

June because she identifies with Henry? Hugo is quite understanding about the romantic permutations but enjoys a moment of revenge after Anaïs leaves Henry in a huff on the night of the Art Students' Ball: amid the carnival taking place in the streets of Paris, he is the masked man who grabs Anaïs from behind and ravishes her.

In another scene of erotic daring, Anaïs and Hugo go to a brothel to watch an "exhibition" of two women making love. Anaïs chooses one who looks like exactly like June and another who resembles herself. When June returns to Paris, she and Anaïs finally consummate their attraction. Throughout the film, writing is a function of the romantic escapades, with Henry trying to finish and then publish *Tropic of Cancer*, while Anaïs composes and embellishes in her diary. Her contact with Henry and June has provided the rite of passage that will make a real writer of her.

Two resonant encounters inform *Henry and June.* Kaufman and his wife met Henry Miller in 1960 at his house in Big Sur, where the writer intrigued them with praise for "'the wonderful, mysterious journals of Anaïs Nin,' which he felt were major works, unseen but by a few friends," Kaufman wrote in an email of February 16, 2002. Miller called them "seminal sexual chronicles of the journeys of a woman's soul, documents of literary times and aspirations" that were "not those of the 'Lost Generation' writers." Kaufman added that the journals began appearing only in the mid 1960s and surmised that that "they were constantly gone over and revised by Anaïs . . . and quite possibly by Hugo and [her executor] Rupert Pole, especially the later ones which appeared after her death in 1977. The volume 'Henry and June,' published in 1986, a short time before we adapted it into film-form, was the 'unexpurgated' diary of Anaïs. So the earlier published versions were 'expurgated' by them . . . probably in order to be published in a 'safe' form."

Kaufman met Anaïs Nin in 1963, when she came to the University of Chicago to present the "underground" films of Ian Hugo, an avant-garde filmmaker. "To my surprise," Kaufman remarked, "Ian Hugo turned out to be none other than Hugo, her husband. I asked her about her journals. My memory is that she was not sure that they'd ever be published." Spending the afternoon with her, Kaufman told her some ideas he had for a film, and Nin provided the encouragement he needed to make his first movie, *Goldstein.* He was later drawn to the "endless weave of mystery" that characterized her life as well as her journals.

"Anaïs, though a near-cult figure to some, was attacked by many critics for taking 'liberties' with the truth, for fabricating," he continued. "While this might have been the case, to us her 'lies' were often an attempt to transcend the 'facts' in order to arrive at 'her truth,' the truth of the heart. The ending to our film was taken from additional 'unexpurgated' journals that went beyond the volume 'Henry and June': these were first published in a quarterly journal called *Anaïs* by Rupert Pole. The scenes—where she goes to bed with June and what follows—were, I believe, later published in the next unexpurgated volume, 'Incest.'"

The film opens with Anaïs's voice and a black screen. We then read, "Paris, 1931," and see a close-up of her eyes being lifted to the camera. This double narration establishes Anaïs visually—seeing and being seen—as well as verbally (unlike the refusal of the spoken word at the beginning of *The Unbearable Lightness of Being*). Her first words, "It all began so innocently," engender the image: a man's voice enters, replacing hers, leading to Anaïs's flashback of discovering erotica in a closet. Although the man to whom Anaïs speaks is a publisher (Jean-Louis Buñuel), the confessions he elicits from her suggest psychoanalysis.[6] As in *The Unbearable Lightness of Being*, the film's first scene depicts two people in an office. Tomas's line, "Take off your clothes," is implied by the way the publisher looks at Anaïs: he is another professional with a subtext of seduction. The voyeurism of doctor and patient in Kaufman's previous film then becomes that of Anaïs looking with intoxication at a box of erotic photos. Given Kaufman's predilection for intricate structuring and visual rhymes, the photographs prepare for subsequent scenes: one is of a semi-naked masked female, and another is of a woman and her reflection—appropriate to a film filled with expressive mirrors. (We might recall Sabina showing Tereza photos by Man Ray in *The Unbearable Lightness of Being*, as we once again see women gazing at other women.) Kaufman often depicts Anaïs seeing what she should not: a man's wallet stolen before her eyes; Henry crying at the movies; their friend Osborn (Kevin Spacey) in bed with three nude women; the brothel Henry enters after she gives him money; Henry and June kissing passionately in the oval mirror of her home; and (in a lyrical subjective shot from her bicycle) a sexual embrace between June and Henry in the woods.

Beginning the film with the eyes of Anaïs introduces the importance of the gaze, both for the character and the audience. We then see her performing, taking a class in Spanish dance while her cousin Eduardo (Jean-Philippe Ecoffey) watches appreciatively. The camera tracks the mirror-lined dance studio behind a window, offering us a mediated perspective.[7] When Anaïs dances for Henry in the nightclub, close-ups of their eyes express their growing passion. Similarly, when Anaïs and Hugo go to the brothel (the same one where she first followed Henry) and they engage in an exhibition, the cross-cutting—from her eyes to those of the prostitute who resembles her—conveys her desire. Moreover, the exhibition turns out be in a mirror, with the prostitutes always internally framed. This expresses how they are reflecting at least two levels: the voyeuristic desires of Anaïs and Hugo in the room, as well as Anaïs's imagining of herself with June. This multiple framing also distances us, reminding us of the film's self-consciousness.

The quotation of movie scenes within *Henry and June* heightens our awareness of the gaze as a charged process of sensual awareness. After

Anaïs (Maria de Medeiros) and her husband Hugo (Richard E. Grant) watch an exhibition of prostitutes in *Henry and June*. (Note the doubled reflection.) Courtesy of Universal Studios.

Henry cries when watching June onscreen, there are clips from three seminal motion pictures: *Maedchen in Uniform* (an early cinematic depiction of lesbian love) prepares for the desire that grows between Anaïs and June; *The Passion of Joan of Arc* returns to the theme of innocence articulated in the opening sequence; and viewers yelling "obscene!" at *Un Chien Andalou* extend the literal and figurative mirrors throughout *Henry and June.*

Reflections are not simply aesthetically compelling; they illustrate the exploration of identity at the heart of the film. Despite the title, *Henry and June* is about Anaïs's rite of passage from innocence to an experience that will make her a better writer. At first, she sees what is forbidden, and later she is looked at by every man in the nightclub. The essence of Anaïs might be, "I am seen; therefore, I am." But Anaïs's identity seems even more a function of her articulation—perhaps, "I write, therefore I am." The constant fading in and out suggests Anaïs posing for the camera, a visual portraiture that represents her verbal efforts. The film celebrates the written word, from the first conversation between Henry and Anaïs about D. H. Lawrence (who is later the subject of a toast) to scenes of passionate writing activity by both. (Henry is writing *Tropic of Cancer,* which would be banned for twenty-seven years in English-speaking countries. In a delightful example of intertextual casting, Bruce Myers plays the man who will publish his work; in *The Unbearable Lightness of Being,* he played the editor of Tomas's article—publishing controversial material in both films.)

Those who can write exert a measure of control—they are, after all, subjects—whereas June is depicted as someone who remains an object. Before we meet her, Henry tells Anaïs that June stole her life from a movie. (The construction of identity is not limited to these writers.) June is first glimpsed in a photo, then in a film—both are mediated frames—and finally appears to us in a visual echo of the introduction of Anna Quadri in *The Conformist*: both Uma Thurman and Dominique Sanda saunter toward the camera with the confidence of being expected. When she first speaks, June has all the insolence of youth, beauty, and Brooklyn. But she later complains about how she is represented. In a telling scene of Anaïs and June reading Henry's unfinished novel, she blurts out, "This isn't me." Henry acknowledges, "Of course—it's the you inside me," as we see June reflected in the mirror. "It's a distortion!" she cries. Unable to write her own book, June is powerless, except insofar as she is desired. As Anaïs's diary entry puts it, "She lives on reflections of herself in others' eyes" (Nin 15). June can toy with a man—as in the scene where she convinces a ticket agent to give her passage to America despite a lack of cash—but her immortality is dependent on those who write about her. (Later, in the same room where June verbally attacked Henry, she gently reproaches Anaïs for how she writes about her as well.) By contrast, Henry controls verbally, often after humiliation. While there is something childish and futile about his throwing paint on June's photo, his words can lash and last.

Visual details express him succinctly. First seen lighting a match on the sole of his shoe for a cigarette, Henry is a rough guy. (As in the opening of *The Unbearable Lightness of Being*, a visual spark leads to provocative images.) Unlike the effete Hugo, he doesn't mind a cockroach on his papers: he flicks a giant one rather than killing it. When served a soufflé for dessert at the home of Anaïs and Hugo, he cuts off the top, conveying not only his lack of gustatory sophistication but his brusque removal of something that rises. The sexual metaphor connects to the flashback scene of Henry spying on June and having his tie caught in the closing window; an image of castration seems appropriate, given that he fears her infidelity. In fact, June often dangles a puppet that resembles Henry: unlike the "Count Bruga" puppet in the book, the film's "Bruga" is even bald like him.

Kaufman's visual storytelling extends to the other major characters as well, heightening Nin's journals. For example, in his car Hugo is obliterated by light behind the windshield, expressing how easily he disappears from Anaïs's gaze. In the final scene, however, after June has disappeared, Anaïs is the one who is visually obstructed when he picks her up in the automobile. (Kaufman often ends his movies with a couple in a car—*The Wanderers, The Unbearable Lightness of Being*, and *Rising Sun*. When this was pointed out to him, he joked, "And maybe *The Right Stuff* would've closed with two guys together in a capsule had there been room." It seems right that Kaufman ends the action on the road: he leaves his characters in motion, implying that their stories continue beyond "The End.") As in *The Unbearable Lightness of Being*, we are occasionally teased by a partial revelation into desiring a fuller view. This is especially true in the love scenes between Anaïs and June. The first one is presented as a dream after Anaïs returns to the brothel (where she exchanges intense looks with the androgynous prostitute who resembles June). Anaïs and June embrace in a dark room that includes a goldfish bowl. Anaïs's voice accompanies the sensuous image, as it turns out that she is narrating the scene to Eduardo (in a room that also contains a goldfish bowl). June's face changes to that of the prostitute, and then back, before we move to the goldfish bowl and the women's reflection. Fluidity informs the content and the style, images gently surging like the bodies of June and Anaïs. When June does return to France towards the end of the film, Anaïs says to her, "Your eyes make me shy" (which is probably less the case for the viewer luxuriating in the sight of their partially disrobed bodies). They make love, tentatively but passionately, until June angrily realizes that Henry and Anaïs have been lovers and runs away.

If the faces of June and the prostitute "rhyme" within a crucial scene, Kaufman's stylistic choices are poetic in rhyming two seductions. Henry first takes Anaïs physically backstage in the nightclub, pulling her to the dark area behind the curtain. "Ya wanna dance?" he asks, almost raping her behind the screen where we see two women dancing, their silhouettes undulating to the Latin music. Anaïs's subsequent arousal of Eduardo in the same locale creates a parallel scene: Henry is not simply her lover but her mentor. Just as he puts up his arm against the wall to stop her, so she raises her arm to her enamored cousin. She stops him in his tracks and leads him to the space behind the female performers, kissing him as the women perform to throbbing music.

The fact that Hugo is playing the drums during the first seduction of Anaïs by Henry dynamically enriches the scene. Kaufman cross-cuts from them to Hugo on the conga drums: the primal sound is a reminder that Hugo is part of the moment, providing the beat. Significantly, the drums are a sound bridge to the next shot of Anaïs's ecstatic face: if we were expecting to see her with Henry, we are surprised that her lovemaking is with Hugo. The editing expresses the intense sexuality that she transfers from her lover to her husband. Anaïs's ability to love more than one person at a time is suggested again by a stylistic detail in the film's final love scene. As Kaufman dissolves from Henry's hand on Anaïs's nipple (in the bedroom) to Hugo's fingers playing a guitar in the garden, we sense how intertwined they are: this is the second time that Hugo might be hiding behind a musical instrument while his wife is in Henry's arms. (Like *The Unbearable Lightness of Being*, the film is structured via a strong triangle, with Hugo and Franz marginalized. But Kaufman renders Hugo a bit more prominent by including him in the background of Anaïs and Henry's caress.)

This scene follows another example of judicious editing that creates both tension and an all-encompassing sensuality. Hugo comes home early, unaware that Henry is in their bedroom, making love to Anaïs (her black lace outfit an emblem of peek-a-boo design). The maid keeps him in the kitchen, where Hugo enjoys a croissant and coffee: the cross-cutting to the intensely aroused lovers makes us wonder—along with the maid—whether they will hear him before being discovered in bed. But it also renders Hugo a continuing presence between them, an implicit part of their love. By the time he comes upstairs, Anaïs is ready to welcome him, alone.

Editing is an integral and self-conscious component in other sequences as well. The abrupt cut from the brothel exhibition to Anaïs dancing with Hugo another night—in a club where she is a magnet to every man's gaze—underlines how she has assumed the exhibitionist role. Montage is also the method for conveying (with a wink) how the great photographer Brassaï set up his images: accompanied by upbeat music, he and his buddies select oversized women of the street and immortalize them in photos. (As in *The Great Northfield Minnesota Raid*, Kaufman delights in representing early photography, including the burst of fire needed for each flash.) The carnival sequence offers the most passionate editing, as elaborately costumed students from the Ecole des Beaux-Arts frolic in the streets of the Left Bank (including many, like Osborn, who are nude). Kaufman cuts from a curious Anaïs strolling amid the revelers to a masked man who is following her. When he grabs her, the cuts—including a bear on a leash, a statue with water coming from its mouth, and a black man playing drums—build in a quickening tempo to a peak of dangerous eroticism. Like Tereza with the engineer in *The Unbearable Lightness of Being*, Anaïs initially fights the rapist but then clasps him . . . even before he says, "Pussy Willow," which we recognize as Hugo's term of endearment for Anaïs. The image is then jittery, as if representing her trembling body.[8] The freedom of the mask feeds into the larger themes of liberation that permeate the film.

Scenes such as these exemplify how Kaufman builds upon the literary text to create an entirely cinematic work of art. This disturbing but exhilarating ball sequence is based on a mere mention in the book (190). Similarly, the film introduces a lesbian bar—unlike the book's less vivid sandal shop—as an appropriate backdrop to June's memorable night in Paris with Anaïs before returning to New York. As they dance together in a kind of intoxication, we see the heady freedom of Paris in the 1930s (including a cameo by Rose Kaufman as the handsome woman who tries to pick up Anaïs). Kaufman does not simply compress the text but creates harmonies throughout the film. The diary's first love scene between Anaïs and Henry takes place in his room, but the film moves the seduction to a nightclub, counterpointed by a performance of female dancers. And if her first sexual moment with Eduardo is in a hotel, the film makes it a reprise of Henry and Anaïs backstage in the club. The exhibition in the book (70) is not a return to Henry's bordello, nor does Anaïs choose a June lookalike; but these changes in the film add deep resonance.

Anaïs Nin's diary provides a literary "voice," as each entry creates a scene. A particularly graphic and unsettling example is her dream of making love to June (91), including goldfish as a metaphor for female genitalia. The film literalizes this element of "voice": she recounts the dream aloud to Eduardo, narrating within the frame. If the book mentions Henry seeing a soufflé for the first time (37), the film takes it further: his inappropriate cutting off the top makes it an example of Henry's American crudeness; moreover, it leads him to exclaim how wonderful the meal is, a moment of sensual appreciation that will be developed in later scenes.

Among the numerous changes from the text is June's attempt to get a steamship ticket with insufficient funds. Nin describes the scene from her own perspective: "We walked into several steamship agencies. June did not have enough money for even a third-class passage and she was trying to get a reduction. I saw her lean over the counter, her face in her hands, appealing, so that the men behind the counter devoured her with their eyes, boldly. And she so soft, persuasive, alluring, smiling up in a secret way at them. I was watching her begging. Count Bruga leered at me. I was only conscious of my jealousy of those men, not of her humiliation" (29). In the film, there is only one man, and June's manipulation of him is successful. Instead of being humiliated, June is shown to be (at least temporarily) in control. This is related to Henry's flashback of him dancing with June: a tilt down to their feet is followed by a tilt back up, but this time June is dancing with a woman named Jean. The film's characters have greater autonomy than the individuals described in Nin's diary. The erotic energy of Kaufman's June—and later of Anaïs—is inclusive, allowing for substitution and displacement (as with the prostitute who resembles June). In wondering about whose sensuality anchors the film, we realize that it shifts: sometimes June is the center, at other moments Anaïs. Ultimately, the book's focus is necessarily verbal—including the letters exchanged by Henry and Anaïs—whereas the film relishes its visual depiction of June, Henry, and Anaïs in physical proximity or contact.

A beautiful description of Anaïs Nin's extended sensuality can be found on page 101: "I have just been standing before the open window of my bedroom and I have breathed in deeply, all the sunshine, the snowdrops, the crocuses, the primroses, the crooning of the pigeons, the trill of the birds, the entire procession of soft winds and cool smells, of frail colors and petal-textured skies, the knotted gray-brown of old trees, the vertical shoots of young branches, the wet brown earth, the torn roots. It is all so savory that my mouth opens, and it is Henry's tongue which I taste, and I smell his breath as he sleeps, wrapped in my arms." For this heightened verbal receptivity to the physical world, the film substitutes scenes like a bicycle-riding jaunt: Anaïs and June pedal faster, their skirts and scarves dancing, overtaking Henry and Hugo on their bikes (reminiscent of a bicycle race in *Jules and Jim*). Another evocative scene presents June and Anaïs romantically dancing together (evoking a similar moment in *The Conformist*).

Among the films that seem to inform *Henry and June* are these two other classic adaptations from literary works: *The Conformist* and *Jules and Jim*. Both are tales of romantic triangles, period reconstructions in which the male characters are ineluctably drawn to riveting, ambiguous women. Of the two, Kaufman articulated a greater awareness of Truffaut's influence when he wrote, "*Jules and Jim* is always in the back of my mind. Truffaut had a wonderfully unique way of being playful and evasive, of finding visuals to convey the charm and thrill of youthfulness." We can compare the ways in which both films depict the desired but unfulfilled woman: Catherine (Jeanne Moreau), like June, is a mysterious and free creature who becomes increasingly uncomfortable with the pedestal on which her lovers place her. *Henry and June* echoes Stanley Kauffmann's wonderful description of *Jules and Jim* as "an isosceles triangle that becomes equilateral" (226).

And just as Truffaut revived the music of the great 1930s French composer Maurice Jaubert in later films such as *The Story of Adele H.*, Kaufman uses French music of the 1930s in a dynamically integrated way, incorporating Jaubert, Stravinsky, and Erik Satie. For example, when Henry rides on his bicycle to Anaïs, we hear a melody from Jean Vigo's classic film of 1934, *L'Atalante*. For viewers who are unfamiliar with the source music by Jaubert, it simply functions as a lighthearted and rhythmic accompaniment; for those who recognize the melody, it is a link to another lyrical cinematic text about a couple who are separated and then reunited. Similarly, during Anaïs's exchange of glances with June's lookalike in the brothel, we hear a famous song of the period, "J'ai deux amours" (diegetically, as we also see the record being played and winding down at the end). "I Have Two Loves" seems like an appropriate title indeed, except that Anaïs's erotic drive cannot be limited to a simple choice: she makes love to at least four different people in the course of the film. Most importantly, *Henry and June* opens with the notes of a bassoon which turn out to be the opening of "The Rite of Spring." This might have been a prescient choice; as Kaufman acknowledged in 2002, "I remember thinking at the time how Stravinsky's work was met with a violent reaction on its first performance; and how both Anaïs and Henry were pilloried and banned in their day. And I kept that in mind when it came to getting the NC-17 rating: it seemed in keeping with Stravinsky's and Anaïs's Rite Stuff."

As the first film to receive the NC-17 rating, *Henry and June* became part of the culture wars in the United States. Certain newspapers would not advertise it, and a few theaters in the South would not play it. Kaufman succeeded on his own terms: he once again provides sophisticated reflection and expression, adapting an erotically charged book with sensuality appropriate to cinema. *Henry and June* extends the exploration in *The Unbearable Lightness of Being* of the erotic aura emanating from a character, so strong that it touches anyone who enters. In the film, Henry

Miller preaches liberation—sexual and literary—with a certain rough-ness; *Henry and June* celebrates sexual and artistic liberation, too—but with a more female sensibility, a fluidity appropriate to its heroine.

This fluidity might also exist in terms of truth or fact. From the very beginning—when Anaïs's voiceover confesses, "I tell Hugo only part of the story"—we wonder which is true: was it "just one kiss," as she tells her husband, or the extended sexual acts that she chronicles in her di-ary? Kaufman acknowledged, "A friend of mine, who knew Anaïs very well, was upset with the revelations in *Henry and June,* which detailed relationships hitherto unrevealed or denied. She was upset with Anaïs's 'lying.' For us, it was those very intriguing lies that led us to want to explore the enigmas of her romantic yearnings. Her 'wanting to be in-nocent' like June, who had tried and explored 'everything' (generally considered the opposite of innocent, no?) might make for an interesting discussion comparing the journeys of Anaïs and the Abbe in *Quills*: the 'innocent' traveling through pain, tragedy, sex, and (hopefully) some laughter on the way to 'becoming an artist.'"

Quills

Quills (2000) may be set in France at the end of the eighteenth century, but its mordantly witty depiction of the Marquis de Sade (1740–1814) offers a cautionary tale for the beginning of the twenty-first century. With a pungent script by Doug Wright (adapted from his Obie Award–winning play of 1995), Kaufman's provocative direction led *Quills* to receive the Best Film of the Year Award from the National Board of Review—an organization that, appropriately enough, champions free-dom of expression. A portrait of the artist as an aging pervert, it also portrays the—albeit extreme—writer as the product of a repressive, violent, and hypocritical society.

The flamboyant Marquis de Sade (Geoffrey Rush, in an Oscar-nom-inated performance) is introduced only twenty minutes into the film, but he is glimpsed in the first sequence, writing pornography behind a window while a beautiful young woman is beheaded by guillotine in 1794 Paris. As children watch the public spectacle, *Quills* suggests that society has no problem with youngsters exposed to violence, and ques-tions whether the Marquis's stories are really worse than the display of bloody dismemberment sanctioned by the government. As Kaufman said in February 2001 at the Philadelphia Weekend Film Festival (where he was honored with a retrospective of his work), "At the beginning we show that if you came to see the Marquis for porn or sexual bondage, you'll see something more pornographic than the Marquis: history." (He also acknowledged that the film's opening could be a warning for some viewers to leave: "Not for children of all ages!" he wrote in the introduction to Fox Searchlight's press kit for *Quills*.)

Sade is later imprisoned in the asylum of Charenton, where we see him through the eyes of two sympathetic characters: the asylum's idealistic supervisor—l'Abbé de Coulmier (Joaquin Phoenix)—believes that his inmates can curb bad behavior by expressing demons in their art, while the laundress Madeleine (Kate Winslet) smuggles out the Marquis's lurid prose. Hence, he is allowed to write—although the Abbé has no idea that Madeleine is a literary go-between, hiding his manuscripts in the sheets—and a pyromaniac paints fire on a canvas. Sade's *Justine* is published anonymously and devoured, till the Emperor Napoleon orders it destroyed. Censorship in the form of book burning only enflames the citizens to buy—or share—surviving copies.

The Marquis de Sade (Geoffrey Rush)
and Madeleine (Kate Winslet) in *Quills*.
Courtesy of Twentieth Century Fox.

Napoleon dispatches Dr. Royer-Collard (Michael Caine) to clamp down on the popular Marquis. A hard-liner and a hypocrite who believes only in control and punishment, the doctor turns out to be far more "sadistic" (despite the origin of the name in Sade) and lethal than the writer. He marries a teenaged virgin from the convent, but Simone (Amelia Warner) won't remain the caged bird that he locks into a bedroom and forces to submit to brutal sex: while secretly reading *Justine,* she seduces the handsome young architect Prouix (Stephen Moyer), whom the doctor hired to make their new home resplendent. The Marquis is comfortably ensconced in the asylum because of his aristocratic wife Renee's influence—better to be considered insane than a criminal—and when Renee (Jane Menelaus, Rush's real-life spouse) attends Charenton's theater production, it is clear she still loves her husband. But the Marquis's short play performed by the inmates brazenly displays his contempt for Royer-Collard: it is a farce about an old doctor who takes a virginal wife from the convent.

Royer-Collard takes his revenge, forcing the Abbé to abet him in taming the naughty celebrity. When his quills and ink are taken away, the Marquis improvises implements, dipping a chicken bone into red wine to compose on a bedsheet. When these are removed, he uses his own blood and a mirror shard, writing on his clothes. After he is left naked and bereft of objects, he dictates to an inmate, who passes the lines on to another inmate, and another, until it reaches Madeleine, who writes the tale on paper. But his bawdy words incite the inmate Bouchon (the executioner of the opening scene), who attacks Madeleine. Royer-Collard allows the climactic rape and murder of the laundress to take place. The distraught Abbé, who considers the Marquis responsible for her death, authorizes the severing of Sade's tongue. The writer's last defiance as an artist is to use his own excrement to write on the walls of the dungeon. His last act as a man is to refuse the Abbé's offer to kiss a small cross; instead, he swallows it . . . death by crucifix in a perverse mirroring of another naked man tortured and killed. (Wright's screenplay adds pungently, "The Marquis has ingested Christ" [*Quills* Polished Draft 107].) In the film's epilogue one year later, Royer-Collard is running the asylum and reaping profits from publishing Sade's work openly: instead of quelling the Marquis's writing, the doctor ends up selling it. The Abbé is now a prisoner in Sade's former cell, begging for a quill and paper. Madeleine's blind mother (Billie Whitelaw) secretly provides them.

Quills opens with the close-up of a beautiful young woman who seems to be expecting her offscreen lover. But Kaufman quickly undercuts our expectations: what seems to be an erotic moment turns out lethal. As in *Rising Sun*, the white female neck poised for an embrace is vulnerable indeed. The dirty fingernails of a man encroach until we realize that he is an executioner; she is about to lose her head literally rather than figuratively. What appeared private is also rendered perversely public: she is on a scaffold, a stage before an audience hungry for blood. "Dear reader," we hear, as the Marquis's voiceover literally invites us in. But if we assumed a coincidence between the tale Sade is telling—about Mlle. Renard's love of pain in sex—and the image before us, we are mistaken. As the classical music rises, a different story unfolds: the relationship between words and pictures is contrapuntal. Whatever the Marquis writes, it will not be as gruesome as the decapitation of a lovely woman. His chained hand dips the quill in red ink: what he composes is therefore the color of the violence around him—not "purple prose," but bloody. The beheading of the female aristocrat reddens the frame, providing a transition to Charenton: the red screen before we hear Madeleine ask, "Your linens please," foreshadows her own gashes during a public whipping, and ultimately her murder at the hands of the same executioner. In this elemental opening—after the intense physicality of the woman's pronounced breathing, the wind in her hair, and the earthy dirt of the executioner's nails—the title of *Quills* appears over water, namely the laundry of Charenton. (Later Napoleon will burn *Justine* in the fireplace.)

Kaufman once again explores voyeurism, beginning with the Marquis behind a window: he is both a spectator to the excesses of the French Revolution and (for us) a spectacle. Moreover, as Lauren Schwartz elaborates in an unpublished essay, the camera seems to be mounted on the guillotine's blade as it falls rapidly onto the female neck: "Suddenly we, the audience, are the guillotine . . . the consumers demanding the violence of this scene, . . . because we . . . pay to see it. In a single shot, Kaufman has both satiated and implicated us as the motivating force behind the woman's execution . . . a perfect realization of our own hypocrisy as both consumers and critics of violent cultural products" (18–19). The self-conscious gaze continues with Madeleine at the window of his cell in Charenton: the camera tracking in to the rectangle turns out to be her point of view. But at other moments, it is not clear whose perspective the heightened camera movement represents. When it glides through the corridors of the asylum, we realize that someone is always watching. "Even the walls have eyes," says Royer-Collard. (The walls have voices, too, during the Marquis's dictation.) A cane thrust into a sculpted eye (part of the statuary on the door of the doctor's new house) reminds us that our sight can be assaulted.

The sumptuous cinematography of Rogier Stoffers foregrounds the surveillance aspect of voyeurism, as in *Rising Sun,* rather than the erotic visual invitations of *The Unbearable Lightness of Being* and *Henry and June.* Kaufman recalled in the press kit of *Quills* the pertinent questions that confronted him in this regard: "How to make this movie? How to transform the theatrical setting to film, how to move the camera so that it constantly might reveal something new as voyeurs and gossips spy upon one another through cracks, crevices, slots, and peepholes? How to find cockeyed angles that might be amusing one moment, terrifying the next?" Not unlike Sade's pornographic tales, the image often de-eroticizes the flesh: for example, the extreme close-up of the Marquis's eye, distorted in a circular window, is less titillation than overripe stylization. "Haven't you ever seen a man naked before?" he says to the camera, before Madeleine is shown at the window.

"Take off your clothes" has a completely different meaning in *Quills* from *Unbearable Lightness,* especially when the stripped object of our gaze is the scrawny Marquis: the Abbé orders him to remove his "text-clothes," which the writer has covered with an obscene tale.[9] Sade turns the scene around, commanding attention by parading his nakedness before the troubled young priest. As Kaufman remarked during our interview at the 2001 Philadelphia Weekend Film Festival, "When Rush's wig is taken away and he's naked, he becomes a modern man."[10] This scene is a culmination of the process of stripping away Sade's possessions. (The depletion of his once-opulent cell coincides with the increasing abundance of the doctor's house.) The Abbé treats Sade like a child, taking away his "toys," but he is not punishable. Even when we later see his severed tongue in a jar, it is phallically upright, a reminder of his virile prose. The Abbé is ultimately no match for the hyper-lucid

Marquis: speaking to him of the virgin birth, Sade dismisses "an entire religion built on an oxymoron." (The Abbé, however, is not off the mark when he exclaims, "You're not the anti-Christ, just a malcontent who knows how to spell.") The placement of the camera is often bracingly expressive, like a shot of the Marquis in his armchair, his hand reaching the floor (as opposed to an earlier shot of Napoleon's feet dangling above the ground). He is big in every sense—riling the doctor, making Madeleine his accomplice, ruffling society's feathers, and finally taking over the Abbé's personality like a dybbuk.

Nevertheless, *Quills* is a kind of quartet, as opposed to the biography of a pornographic writer who was the naughty rock star of his day (Kaufman likens Sade to Mick Jagger). Each of the four major characters is strong-willed and compelling, asserting what he or she believes. The screenplay even calls the Marquis and the doctor "doppelgangers" when "a flicker of recognition passes between them" (Wright, *Quills* Polished Draft, 21). The Abbé is a man of the Enlightenment who trusts that the making of art can be compensatory. But does an inmate exorcise his demons or simply exercise them when he commits them to paper? Does the Marquis, for example, rein them in, or give them reign? Madeleine suggests that its reception can be compensatory too when she says she finds salvation from her drudgery in reading. But the complexity of *Quills* comes from its acknowledgment that art can indeed be dangerous. When the Marquis, deprived of all writing instruments, dictates a story—relayed in a chain by inmates through holes in prison walls—the effect is literally incendiary. The pornographic words lead the pyromaniac to set fire to the chateau, and the executioner to rape and kill. Then again, the film proposes that the only ones incited by the Marquis's story are the "insane," as opposed to average readers. Moreover, the manner of the story's transmission is like the "telephone" game played by children: as Sade's words are repeated from one inmate to another, they are comically simplified. "To my beloved reader, prepare yourself for the most impure tale every to spring from the mind of man" becomes—in the mouth of the third transmitter—"Prepare yourself, I've a tale, an impure tale." The Marquis's line, "with that, Fauchon expelled a scream so extravagantly pitched," is reduced, a few inmates later, to, "with that, the extravagant bitch screamed so loud. . . ."

Sade is less a degenerate scribbler than an unsparing intimator of people's darker urges. Because he intuits that the Abbé loves Madeleine, chafing at his vows of chastity, he taunts him. This culminates in the disturbing dream sequence of the young priest embracing Madeleine's corpse: she seems to suddenly come alive, responding sexually to the repressed and grief-stricken Abbé. But when he lifts himself off her body, she is once again dead, and he seems undone. (The stage version extends the fantasy, with Madeleine as a devilish tease that the priest manages to resist.) We next see him in the film's circular ending: the Abbé wears Sade's ring and hums his tune in a kind of identity transfer.

The melody could not be more appropriate. The Marquis hums the famous French ditty "Au clair de la lune" after hearing it sung by the children who witness the opening decapitation. Its innocent sound is a counterpoint to the savagery around them, while the lyrics foreshadow the Marquis's subsequent predicament in Charenton:

> Au clair de la lune [By the light of the moon],
> Mon ami Pierrot [My friend, little Peter],
> Prête-moi ta plume [Lend me your quill]
> Pour écrire un mot [To write a word].
> Ma chandelle est morte [My candle is dead],
> Je n'ai plus de feu [The fire has gone out].
> Ouvre-moi ta porte [Open your door]
> Pour l'amour de Dieu [For heaven's sake].

The song conveys Kaufman's take on *Quills* as a "fable, like Grimm's fairy tales of horror such as 'Hansel and Gretel' or 'Little Red Riding Hood.' We were given dark images to grow up on; maybe they helped us grow up," the director added.[11]

Whether musically or cinematographically, the film's self-conscious flourishes remind us that *Quills* is invented rather than historically accurate. On the one hand, the filmmakers made sure to get visual details right, studying paintings by artists from Ingres to Van Eyck. "We tried for the shadings and dark tones of Dutch masters (Rogier Stoffers, being from Amsterdam, was bred on brooding tones)," Kaufman explained. "But where they often opted for the darker browns and sepias, we pushed the film more into the green shades (appropriate for the dank, moldy environs of Charenton). We suspected that some of the Dutch masters had used more of these greenish tints, but that these were now lessened by fading and varnishes, the ravaging of time and tide. Chardin's still lifes, on occasion, were in this greener tone, as were some of the paintings by Louis Leopold Boilly. And of course, David, painting at the time of *Quills,* was a prime influence."[12] But in terms of fidelity to fact, the filmmakers took liberties galore. The actual Abbé was a far-from-handsome dwarf (Goodman 20). The real Madeleine was not a virgin; in fact, her mother approved of the Marquis paying for her sexual favors (Sragow, "Return"). In the *Washington Post,* Stephen Hunter pointed out that Sade was sentenced to death in 1772, before the revolution (while calling *Quills* "profane, sacrilegious, pornographic, sadistic, and Sade-istic, titillating, and the most honorable movie of the year" [1]). And the Marquis died of respiratory failure rather than the ingestion of a crucifix.

While *Quills* is faithful to the spirit of Wright's play, it is a boldly cinematic reinvention of an inherently theatrical work of art. The film project did not originate with Kaufman; rather, he was surprised to receive from Fox Searchlight a magnificent screenplay for which he turned out to be wonderfully suited: "I got the script and heard the muffled voice of Geoffrey Rush trying to get out," he recalled. (Kate Winslet was the first actor to commit to the project, however.) He kept Wright on set for the full four weeks of shooting, continually refining the script's transformation of a play into a motion picture. He even sat in on the weeks of rehearsal that preceded the shoot, during which the actors' improvisation was encouraged. As Wright recalled in the press kit, "He helped turn my speeches into visual rhapsodies, and constantly expanded my sense of possibility." The opening sequence, for example, is an intensely cinematic "prologue" and a departure from the stage version, which began with Royer-Collard at Charenton, already married (to "a woman of considerable appetites"), receiving the distraught wife of the Marquis: sick of being called "Satan's bride," she wants her husband silenced (Wright, *Quills,* 165).

Acts 1 and 2 consist primarily of vivid dialogue, in which each character uses words to explain, provoke, or manipulate. We see neither Napoleon nor the performance of the play by Charenton's inmates; Mme. Royer-Collard does not read *Justine;* Renee does not visit her husband in his cell; and there is no scene of Royer-Collard ignoring the cries of Madeleine being attacked by Bouchon. The destruction of

Sade is more grisly than in the film, culminating in death by guillotine. But even before Sade's head is severed, the Abbé gives Royer-Collard a few boxes containing the Marquis's amputated body parts. The play ends with a theatrical flourish in Sade's former room, where the Abbé calls for a quill. The boxes of the Marquis's limbs suddenly open: his amputated hands clap, and his disembodied head tells a new tale. The sound of laughter fills the asylum's halls, but no laundress brings the Abbé a quill.[13] It is fitting that the film ends with Madeleine's mother providing the Abbé with a quill: although a secondary character, she emerges as an audience surrogate. Mme. Leclerc is hardly the only character in the film who—despite a veneer of revulsion upon hearing the Marquis's tales—intones, "Tell me more."

In his introduction to the published version of the play, Wright recalls the "maddening inconsistency" that he discovered in Sade's prose: "One minute it is puerile, moronic, and sex-obsessed as the most irresponsible pornography; the next, it is excoriating and hilarious, its targets worthy, and its barbs as well aimed as those of Jonathan Swift" (xix).[14] Rather than using the original tales, Wright rose to the occasion of composing the Sade stories for *Quills*, penning a purple prose that wittily pays homage to the Marquis.

Even if the film finds its voice in Wright's conception and language, *Quills* bears resemblances to many aspects of Kaufman's other work, particularly *The Unbearable Lightness of Being* and *Henry and June*. The heroines are fearlessly curious; for example, Madeleine discovering the Marquis's erotica rhymes with the first scene of *Henry and June*, in which Anaïs recalls being fascinated by the sexually explicit images she finds in a closet. As Henry Miller is seen mainly through Anaïs's eyes, the Marquis is perceived via Madeleine and the Abbé. And, like Tomas in *Unbearable Lightness*, he is a sexual libertine who is punished more for what he writes than what he does. His use of mirror shards to create his text is reminiscent of the female characters in *Unbearable Lightness*: Sabina's sculptures are made of glass fragments, while Sade's placing shards under his fingertips to make "blood-ink" recalls the nightmare that Tereza recounts to Tomas of piercing her fingers with glass to make the physical agony stop the pain in her heart.

In addition to intertextual reverberations, *Quills* has a curious resonance in terms of political context. Just as the film version of *Marat/*

Sade—Peter Brook's 1966 adaptation of Peter Weiss's play, also set in Charenton—captured the anarchistic spirit of the late 1960s, *Quills* reflects Kaufman's acknowledgment, "I came upon the project at the time of Clinton, Monica Lewinsky, and Kenneth Starr." He likened Royer-Collard to the famed prosecutor, "publishing what he fought against and making 'penis' the most famous word in the English language." Michael Wilmington's laudatory review of *Quills* in the *Chicago Tribune* seizes on the film's topicality: "[W]e must protect ourselves from the Royer-Collards, hypocritical, opportunistic, self-proclaimed guardians of public virtue" (1). Wilmington concludes that *Quills* ranks with such "celebrated, savagely beautiful '60s celebrations of life's wilder side as *Bonnie and Clyde* and *The Wild Bunch*—where the outlaws and their violence expose how fragile and false some of our institutions can be. Like Kaufman, I don't believe in censorship, and I do believe that lies and tyranny rot the soul and corrode lives more surely than any dirty book. That is why his Marquis de Sade—voluptuary in chains, monster of genius and writer without quills—is a figure both comic and tragic, a lost soul trapped between a 'heaven' of vice and a hell of pious brutality" (1).

A comparison with the French drama *Sade* (2002) is instructive, as the focus of Benoit Jacquot's film is quite different. Starring Daniel Auteuil in the title role, it takes place during the French Revolution, when our libertine is imprisoned by the Jacobins in a country estate, a barless jail for aristocrats that looks like a killing field once the guillotine is moved from Paris to its grounds. This Sade is a sly, articulate, and charming atheist, with little trace of the dark mysteries percolating under Rush's wig. (No wig here.) Writing in the *New York Times,* Marcelle Clements astutely outlined the contrasts: "*Quills* is about insanity, creativity and deception, and Mr. Rush's Anglo-Saxon Sade is manic, magnetic and terrifying. Mr. Auteuil's Sade is not crazy—he is anxious and melancholy, burdened by his fame. The Anglo-Saxon Sade is megalomanical and complex but understandable. The French Sade is almost comically arrogant, closed, perversely unfathomable. . . . The Anglo-Saxon Sade is phallic, dynamic, brutal, concupiscent, histrionic—he is an uncontrollable, overpowering proto–sex maniac. The French Sade is more feminine, oblique, nuanced, conflicted. The Sade as imagined by Mr. Jacquot is the modern, re-envisioned Sade, the Sade who is capable of great delicacy, the Sade who was freed by the revolution and briefly became a judge. (He refused to impose the death penalty and was therefore jailed again for the crime of 'modernisme'" [23]).[15]

Of the two films, *Quills* is not only more narratively dramatic and dynamically stylized but a deeper exploration of the artist's role in society. It elaborates on the triangle so often found in Kaufman's films: however, rather than merely romantic, the form conveys a philosophical tension among the three "points" of priest, scientist, and artist (who is the source of conflict between the other two). Wright proposes a corollary in his introduction to the published version of the play when he discusses Sade and Royer-Collard: "[T]he censor has always been the artist's most reliable muse; there is nothing more seductive or inspiring you can say to a would-be provocateur than 'Don't do that'" (xx). Even more than the stage version, Kaufman's film presents numerous visions of art, from the "sanctioned" bust and painting of Napoleon to the subversive *Justine,* under whose influence Simone seduces the architect hired by her husband. The fact that the inmates' choir sings beautifully fulfills the Abbé's view of art as compensatory; but the play they perform—a distorting mirror about an old doctor and his teenage convent bride—wreaks havoc. Sade's tales can be both liberating and incendiary. "Art should raise questions, be resonant, and come up in your dreams," Kaufman concluded. In the Marquis's refusal of hypocrisy, questioning of why violence is sanctioned while sex is taboo (an ongoing reality in how films are rated), and insistence on freedom of expression, Sade may be a paradoxical hero for our own time and place.

Male Relationships and Codes of Honor

From the 1970s into the early 1980s, Kaufman's cinema examined camaraderie, conflicts, and codes of honor among men, whether riding horses and firing weapons in *The Great Northfield Minnesota Raid,* riding spaceships and orbiting the earth in *The Right Stuff,* or hunting whales and surviving the Arctic in *The White Dawn.* Along with the Bronx street-gang setting of *The Wanderers,* they provide him with an opportunity to explore not only heroism—male and flawed—but representation, or how events become legends. After Kaufman left Harvard Law School, he began working on a Ph.D. in American history. Instead of completing a doctorate, however, he wrote the screenplay for *The*

Great Northfield Minnesota Raid in 1968 and turned it into his first serious commercial film by 1972.

The Great Northfield Minnesota Raid

Based on the true story of the Jesse James gang, the film's action unfolds almost one hundred years earlier, in the post–Civil War Missouri of 1876. Since it was made during the Vietnam War, *The Great Northfield Minnesota Raid* (1972) reflects on past and present American history. Kaufman's style is gutsy in its deglamorizing realism; unlike most Westerns up to this time, it glorifies neither the cowboy nor violence. His focus is not the famous hothead Jesse James (Robert Duvall) but the cool and introspective Cole Younger (Cliff Robertson), who expresses "wonderment" about what he sees, from horseless buggies to a steam-powered calliope.

Even though the Missouri legislature votes to give the James and Younger brothers amnesty, Pinkerton's chief detective (Herbert Nelson) is hell-bent on destroying these popular heroes. "Legislators are here to make laws. We're here to make examples," he declares (foreshadowing the doctor who imposes his control in *Quills*). His armed men remain on their trail and shoot Cole after using prostitutes as bait. While Cole is healed by an old woman's magic, Jesse and his gang ride out to attempt a bank robbery in Northfield. Cole and his men try to prevent the heist, but when they learn that the amnesty has been rescinded, Cole enacts a shrewd plan to fill the Northfield bank with money to steal. But the initial euphoria as they convince the townsmen to put their money in the bank—because they fear robbers—gives way to failure before a time-controlled vault. Jesse gratuitously begins shooting, and they are captured. At the end, a bloody Cole, being transported to jail, staggers to his feet and is applauded by crowds. The voiceover tells us that Cole was locked up for twenty-five years. But, as Michael Dempsey wrote in *Film Quarterly* in 1972, a "synopsis takes no account of the swarming minor characters who bounce around inside the film's narrative pinball machine. Kaufman so packs the movie with gunfights, robberies, schemes, chases, a baseball game, a parade, and sundry other incidents that the complexity of the story becomes comic in itself, enhancing the movie's feisty, carnival-like atmosphere. The film gives realism its due—the streets and buildings are resolutely unglamorous, the outlaws ragged and raunchy—but its goggle-eyed energy and mock-dime-novel ambience lift it above mere documentary reconstruction" (48).

The Great Northfield Minnesota Raid opens with a rapid voiceover: "Even before the wounds of the Civil War had healed in Missouri, the railroads came swarming in to steal the land. Everywhere, men from the railroads were driving poor, defenseless families from their homes. And that's when a fresh wind suddenly began to blow." It introduces photographs of the outlaws, creating a historical realism that includes superimposition of black-and-white archival footage on a map—which is torn by the gang as it breaks through the image. This concern with representation is later developed when a photographer tells an undertaker to say "cheese," framed between two upright bodies in caskets. Before meeting Jesse, we see his image on a poster in the Pinkerton detective's hand. The legendary cowboy is introduced in an outhouse, where he and his brother Frank (John Pearce) spit, talk, and defecate together. Sheets of newspaper left on the wall by Cole have both an immediate function and a symbolic one. This primitive version of toilet paper alerts Jesse to the wealth in Northfield; it also reminds the viewer of the ephemerality of the "news"—the public record is reduced to the most private of hygienic acts. Kaufman cuts from one kind of hole to another as Cole is asked by a little boy to show him his bullet wounds. (Children and violence will be linked again in the opening of *Quills*.) The holes in Cole's vest are then rhymed by the outhouse circle from which Jesse peers.

The self-conscious camera work of *The Great Northfield Minnesota Raid* coexists with a gritty authenticity, much like Robert Altman's *McCabe and Mrs. Miller* (shot at the same time, although released in 1971). But Kaufman's vision refuses the poetic grandeur of the West, perhaps because this is the Midwest, industrial and grimy.[16] Beginning in a sepia tone, he retains the look of the past throughout, including numerous dissolves. On the one hand, he uses striking shots, such as handheld camera work during the robbery, or a zoom-in to a calliope in the street from Cole's point of view, or a distorted subjective angle after the ambush. On the other hand, from the introduction of Jesse in an outhouse, naturalistic detail abounds. For example, the men bathe together, trying to rid themselves of the grime often absent from traditional Westerns. Many scenes take place in the rain; one of the gang,

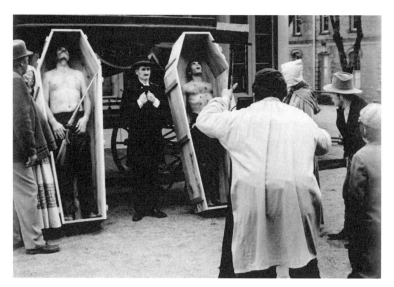

The undertaker poses proudly with the outlaws'
corpses in *The Great Northfield Minnesota Raid.*
Courtesy of Universal Pictures.

Jim Younger (Luke Askew), wears a scarf over his mouth to cover a
disfigurement; and a lengthy baseball game is played on mud and shit.
These details render the film more of a "revisionist Western," revising
our assumptions about the supposedly noble life of cowboys.

It offers a divergent take from previous Hollywood treatments of
the mythic outlaw. For example, the 1939 *Jesse James*—directed by
Henry King from Nunnally Johnson's script—glorifies Tyrone Power's
handsome Jesse as well as Henry Fonda's Frank James. The audience
roots for their freedom, since they are introduced as victims of the
greedy, corrupt representatives of the railroad that is dispossessing the
people. (Jane Darwell, who would play Fonda's mother in *The Grapes of
Wrath*, is the maternal figure here as well, creating a sympathetic family
portrait from the first scene.) *The True Story of Jesse James* (1957)—the
remake directed by Nicholas Ray—is filled with Hollywood clichés,
from clean-cut Robert Wagner and Jeffrey Hunter as the brothers to a
focus on Jesse's romance with his cousin Zee (Hope Lange). The narrative structure is provided by flashbacks from the perspective of their

loyal mother (Agnes Moorehead): she tries to convince the judgmental reverend (John Carradine, who played Robert Ford in the 1939 version) that Jesse is not evil.

The only maternal figure in *Northfield* is the "doll lady" whom Jesse calls "Mother." While he initially treats her reverently, he then kills the elderly woman and escapes in her clothes. The film's other female characters are sympathetic prostitutes. In fact, their introduction provides a link to the opening of two later Kaufman films, *Quills* and *Twisted*: the women call to Cole from a window, but what seems to be erotic turns out to be lethal. We see that a gun is being held to a naked prostitute's head and that the Pinkerton men are using them to lay a trap for Cole.

Kaufman acknowledged that his visual style was designed partly in response to other movies: "What is missing in most of those big Hollywood spectacle pageant films and Westerns is the 'dumbness' of history, the stupidity of the players, their lack of insight, foresight, and sense of humor. In reality, more often than not, the good guys end up in cages, filled with bullets—truth and horror revealed to them too late. Accordingly, I tried to frame shots with that 'dumbness' we see in black and white photos of the period. People are cut off at the edges of frame, and sometimes there's a stiffness to the postures—as with the coffin photography, where the bloody and the brutal are what people value and proudly pose for."

The sound track is equally expressive, from the Scandinavian accents of secondary characters to the bell tolling when a mortician walks by. Often, Dave Grusin's percusssive, upbeat music prepares for the tonal change of scenes, like Jesse's prayer becoming a hoop as they set off for Northfield, or the transition from the shootout to Jesse escaping in drag. Kaufman's addition of a calliope to the robbery sequence creates a mounting aural tension. Standing in the street before the bank, this instrument ends up functioning like a siren, alerting the citizens to disorder inside the vault. Moreover, the ever-curious Cole expresses "wonderment" about Alexander Graham Bell patenting a device for voice transmission. And when he says about the steam engine, "Ain't that a wonderment," he may be expressing Kaufman's own ongoing fascination with technology.

As the director admitted, "Cole Younger was the 'discovery' of the film. Curious about the mechanical world coming into being, he wanted to move forward in time. He was a humanist, a visionary, the true leader of the gang. Had the tragic ending not occurred, history might have remembered him as a better example of a 'hero.' However, it was Jesse and Frank who went on to immortality." Cole has his eye on the future. His heroic possibilities come to the fore when he makes a mustache for the cowboy who is ashamed of his mouth, or a rifle adjustment for the ocularly challenged "Four Eyes." "The national sport is shooting and always will be," he declares prophetically. Even if he is a flawed hero—shooting a baseball, for example—Cole is clearly preferable to Jesse, whose evangelical fervor suggests a truly deranged individual. (Duvall's incantations prefigure his character twenty-five years later in *The Apostle*, which he directed in 1997.) "That blinky-eyed bastard," says Cole about Jesse. "Even his 'vision' ain't his own." Mired in the Civil War past, Jesse rants about Yankees. And when he tells his guys not to allow someone to identify you as a guerilla in enemy territory, he invokes the Vietnam War. Indeed, his railing against northerners is appropriate not only to the post–Civil War context but to Vietnam as well.

Jesse alludes to Quantrill's raiders—Bushwhackers also depicted in Ang Lee's *Ride with the Devil* (1999)—and "Mustache" was shot by a Bushwhacker. Vietnam thus hovers behind the action of *Northfield*, right up to the last scene of Cole in a cell on wheels, invoking Vietnamese prisoners of war. Even the failed enterprise of robbing the Northfield bank can be seen as a reference to the U.S. military presence in Vietnam. And in Pinkerton's chief detective, we perceive a corporate impulse: buying politicians, he cares most about his image.

Among corrupt politicians, Cole and Jesse are popular outlaws, counterculture heroes of their time. But Kaufman distinguishes between them:

> My approach to Jesse James ran counter to the feelings of many of my "antiwar" pals who wanted him to retain his icon status as leader of a "guerilla" movement. In the sixties (and maybe to this day) it was fashionable to think that anyone who was a "guerilla" was automatically good. To say otherwise was, in some circles, "to betray the Movement." That song is over, but its melody lingers on.
>
> This romanticized history of the James gang (remember Tyrone Power/Henry Fonda) was not what I found in my readings. The real Jesse was a self-glorifying, vengeful "blinky-eyed bastard" who would

stop at nothing to perpetuate the war (the unholy cause of the South) and his own myth, a true reactionary in revolutionary disguise.

Kaufman's Jesse rationalizes his robberies as military attacks on the treacherous Yanks (especially because the banks were often owned by northeners). He is also a racist: when he and Frank enter Northfield, reminiscing about a raid, Frank says of the victims that there were no women or children. "At least none of them white," Jesse adds. And his attitude toward women is ambiguous. He is judgmental about the men going to a brothel. And while he seems affectionate to the old woman who shelters them and shows the men her "children"—a collection of dolls—and even calls her "Mother," he reminds his brother that she is a Yank and ultimately kills her.

Northfield was so different from a commercial hit like *Butch Cassidy and the Sundance Kid* (1969) that it could not be marketed as a "feel-good" Western. It now seems closer to the viscerally demystifying portraits of the late 1960s, like *Bonnie and Clyde* (1969) and *The Wild Bunch* (1969). (Kaufman received a Writers' Guild of America nomination for his screenplay.) And, like the end of *Easy Rider* (also 1969), it suggests that ordinary folk can be as lethal as outlaws. Kaufman cast a Pinkerton lookalike in the role of one of Northfield's "good citizens": dressed in a fur coat, he becomes the self-appointed, self-righteous leader of the posse after the bungled robbery. When they search for the thieves in the local brothel, the men take—and hang—four men even if they are not the robbers. And they proceed to shoot at a group who turn out to be another posse searching for Jesse.

Even if the studio did not know what to do with it (and delayed the film's release for a year), a few critics responded enthusiastically. Stephen Farber, for example, called it "a rich mother lode of Americana, with a vivid gallery of characters worthy of Dickens or Twain" (26). On the occasion of the film's DVD release in 2007, Michael Sragow praised how Kaufman "squeezes as much drama, meaning, pictorial beauty, and fun as he can out of their exploits, and glues your attention to the bouncing ball of his narrative. He establishes a formal period look that pays semi-satiric homage to nineteenth-century graphics, then rips right through it with the speed and thump of his action. Kaufman's movie isn't just about the demise of an outlaw gang; it's also about the end of an era of superstition and myth" (Sragow, "Critic's Picks"). *The Great Northfield Minnesota Raid* remains a remarkable amalgam of two time periods, reflecting on the overlap between the Civil War and the Vietnam War. "What I was concerned about at the time, and have come to be increasingly concerned with to this day," said Kaufman, "is that messy-Jesse-messianic ideal wherein a neurotic, self-serving, self-glorifying leader hijacks his own comrades and leads them to their destruction whilst he, the criminal instigator of terrible crimes, goes merrily on his way . . . to be canonized by future historians, songwriters, journalists, and Hollywood mythmakers."

Gavin Smith offers a perceptive overview of a prime dialectic in the director's work: "Kaufman usually focuses on some heroic archetype at the verge of historical extinction, its exemplars trying to do what they do best in a changing world. . . . This applies even to two films he wrote but did not direct, *The Outlaw Josey Wales* and *Raiders of the Lost Ark*. How aware these assorted artists, eccentrics, and adventurers are of their imminent obsolescence varies according to their proximity to the landscape of genre. The closer they are, the more acute the perception" ("Heroic Acts" 36).

The White Dawn

This intriguing adventure drama is set in 1896, twenty years after the time period of *Northfield*. With a screenplay adapted by James Houston, Tom Rickman, and the producer Martin Ransohoff from Houston's novel, it is the first of Kaufman's films to focus on explorers or "wanderers" encountering different cultures. Here, three Americans find themselves among the Eskimo people of the Canadian Arctic. Unlike most Hollywood films of the time, *The White Dawn* (1974) subtitles the Inuit cast members' dialogue rather than having them speak primitive English. *The White Dawn* was also Kaufman's first collaboration with the gifted cinematographer Michael Chapman, who would go on to shoot *Invasion of the Body Snatchers*, *The Wanderers*, and *Rising Sun*.

With dogs and sleds, Eskimos rescue three exhausted whalers, whose boat ran aground and splintered in the ice: Billy (Warren Oates) is greedy, bossy, and disrespectful of the saviors; Daggett (Timothy Bottoms) is kind and able to adapt to the Eskimos' lifestyle, especially when the chief shares one of his wives with him; and Portagee (Louis Gossett Jr.) is a double outsider, a Caribbean black man among whites, and then distinct from Canadian Eskimos. At first, they experience otherness and paranoia (looking forward to Kaufman's *Invasion of the Body Snatchers*, as they worry about cannibalism—being swallowed up or possessed). When the entire group travels to a warmer area, Billy convinces Daggett and Portagee to steal the Eskimos' boat and fish in order to get back to civilization. But they are stranded on an ice floe, rescued by an Eskimo on a kayak, and brought back to the now-starving community. Surprisingly, the Eskimos do not blame the three thieves, instead returning to their winter space and building an igloo together "so souls can dance away the cold." After a ritualistic orgy, Billy makes an alcoholic beverage from berries, leading the Eskimos to get drunk. The consequences are fatal when a young woman staggers naked into the snow and dies. Finally, the community revolts, killing Billy and Portagee. The sympathetic Daggett is protected by the chief's son, but he is ultimately killed as well.

The White Dawn opens on a dual axis, which is not limited to image and sound. The first is historical—"So ends this day," intones the male voiceover narration, from a captain's log of May 13, 1896, as we see a black-and-white map—and the second is elemental, with the vast icy horizon gleaming in color. In the opening sequence, a boat with six men leaves the large ship in pursuit of a whale, which they harpoon. Despite the imminent threat of ice, Billy refuses to cut the line. The voiceover returns, now from May 17, lamenting that the men are lost. Billy is thus established as a dubious leader, but the hierarchy of the nautical code mandates that his orders be followed. As Portagee says later in the film, "Billy, you're gonna kill us all." We see the hubris of men who kill a whale—only to be destroyed by it. The historical realism is reminiscent of *Northfield*, given the shared maps and iris shots. Indeed, Kaufman acknowledged, "Since I had been denied my black-and-white opening on *Northfield* (where I was forced to put colored maps over my hand-cranked-camera black-and-white opening because the studio yelled, 'The audience would turn off black and white if they saw it on TV'), I now seized on the opportunity to get a black-and-white opening on this film. I also felt that the black-and-white added the proper historical authenticity under the captain's log."

Joy Gould Boyum's review of *The White Dawn* in the *Wall Street Journal* compares it with the antecedent of Robert Flaherty's *Nanook of the North,* suggesting that it goes "perhaps one step further than most current films utilizing these verite techniques. For here the documentary aspects not only serve to authenticate a drama but make for its very essence" (8).

The external frame consists of archival footage, a map, a voice, and traditional music. Dates and facts make us aware of the need to record, measure, and articulate. Color enters only a few minutes later for the credit sequence, in which Eskimos in animal furs find and save the three survivors. As the camera tracks in exhilarating lateral movements, we hear a blend of whales and wind, along with percussion accompanying the dogs. This internal frame of ice, dogs, and drums offers a timeless depiction that has no reference points—the snow and the sky seem continuous—and corresponds to the speculative mode: what might have happened to the lost men? The elemental imagery of ice and snow is appropriate to an exploration of the precarious balance of the individual and the community.

Timothy Bottoms (left background), Louis Gossett Jr. (foreground), and Warren Oates (right backround) in *The White Dawn.* Courtesy of Paramount Pictures.

This includes the balance between the animal and the human. The furs worn by all the characters suggest a natural and necessary shading in this primitive landscape: men don't merely look like animals but must behave like them. When the hunters approach a walrus, they are on all fours. "Dog children" is the term used by the Eskimo for the Americans, "half-man, half-dog." But the dog is revered in this culture; after all, dogs really rescue the men. (Nevertheless, the other three Americans who die at the beginning are probably eaten by dogs. And there is a purposefully ambiguous cut from Daggett asking, "Where's Billy? What do you think they did to him?" to a shot of dogs eating bloody meat.) The whale at the beginning is not successfully captured, but Daggett helps the Eskimos pull a seal from under the ice. The Shaman is presented as a fanged monster (reminiscent of a figure with antlers in the large igloo). In one of the film's most remarkable scenes—heightened by the sound of dogs barking—the leader Sarkak (Simonie Kopapik) confronts a polar bear, bravely, determinedly, and ritualistically. Kaufman confided that the bear was flown in from the Seattle Zoo and described the shooting pungently:

> First, the master shot: Sarkak, knife tied to the end of a spear, attacks the bear. The object of this shot is to get them both into the same frame, define the "playing field," and then finish the scene off in close-ups. On "action," everything started out fine, but then terror struck. Just as our polar bear had never seen snow before and had responded with atavistic glee, so too our old Eskimo chief, once a great hunter, had not seen a polar bear so close in many years. And his atavistic glee took over; his dander was up. When he reached the spot where I had drawn a line in the snow, I yelled "cut!" But the old guy didn't stop. He forgot he was in film! He just kept marching toward the bear. Maybe he thought I meant something else by "cut"! The bear reared onto his hind legs—he was about eight or nine feet tall—and let out a chilling roar. I yelled "cut!" I yelled "stop!" And I yelled, "NOOO!" But old Sarkak lunged and poked that bear in the belly with the fake knife at the end of the spear. The bear let out a sort of "ooof" sound and fell docilely onto all fours. It was sort of like Ali/Liston: the crowd was silent. Only then did old Sarkak stop, his blood-lust satisfied. Rifles were lowered. A limp fire extinguisher dripped into the snow. Fortunately the cameraman had kept shooting, and we got that part in one take.

One of the film's most chilling invocations of animals is when the chief later calls the Americans "ravens" because they bring death. (In James Houston's novel, Portagee and Daggett are called "a giant black raven and a nervous white sea gull . . . tall frightening birds" [22], while Billy is compared to a wolf [105].)

Although Billy dismissively says of their rescuers at the beginning, "They're just savages," an Eskimo's subsequent remark to his compatriot, "These people are living with savages," refers to the Americans as primitive. To invoke *Northfield,* Billy is like Jesse James—especially when he mutters, "Damn heathens"—while Daggett's openness is closer to Cole Younger's "wonderment," particularly when he shows his drawings of their whale hunt to the Eskimos. Whereas the chief generously shares his wife Neevee (Pilitak) with Daggett, Billy is possessive. Indeed, if one can compare the Eskimos' simple and harmonious world to a Garden of Eden, Billy is the snake that introduces sin, whether in the form of betrayal by theft or death by liquor. *The White Dawn* thus celebrates the organic existence of the Eskimos, unified by ritual. It continues Kaufman's image in *Northfield* of an old toothless woman's incantation to heal an injured man. (This song, an Inuit chant, is also a bridge to *The Right Stuff,* the basis for the orchestral suite accompanying the astronauts' flight.)

Sound is an important narrative device throughout *The White Dawn,* from the opening counterpoint of wind and whale, to Portagee's playful locomotive noises when Daggett shares his drawings of a train with the Eskimos, to the haunting shot of two young women blowing on each other's vocal cords during the orgy scene. As the novel describes the sisters Evaloo and Mia, one "played on her sister's throat cords and set up a haunting rhythm that once heard could never be forgotten" (Houston 169). The enhanced quick breathing plus percussion is repeated when Daggett is chased to his death at the end. The woman he has grown to love, Neevee, cannot accept his murder: her cry continues after he is killed, piercing the empty landscape. Her solitary voice is quite distinct from an earlier scene in which Portagee creates harmony with the old woman's melody. *The White Dawn* ends with a reprise of this harmony—a musical intertwining that adds Western harmony to primitive monotone, yoking together male and female, Eskimo and American.

Because Henry Mancini's music is used sparingly, it is extremely effective throughout the film.

It contributes to the repetitive structure of *The White Dawn*, which presents two boat trips to a new camp (the second muted) and two manifestations of the Shaman. This is true to the cyclical, seasonal experience of the Eskimos. Daggett's story, however, shares with Kaufman's films such as *The Northfield Minnesota Raid*, *The Unbearable Lightness of Being*, and *Quills* a movement toward the martyrdom of an engaging man. (Daggett's death by arrow is the most horrifying of the three, since it follows that of Billy by knife and Portagee by harpoon.) Similarly, the antagonist is linked to violent greed and consumption: Billy's main question about a fur is how much it will fetch, for example. In his very name is will, which he imposes on others.

While it takes will, of course, to direct a motion picture too, Kaufman's recollections of the shooting focus on the "totally collaborative experience with the Inuit people." Whereas he originally planned to bring professional actors to the Arctic for all but the three leads, he ended up casting locals:

> The Eskimos turned out to be natural actors. They had grown up in a storytelling culture (I wonder if the ensuing years of "modernization"—TV, candy, liquor—since we were there have diminished their storytelling abilities), and they were wonderful visual artists. On top of that, they had what I consider the requisite for any great actor—a great sense of humor. Much of our very difficult physical shooting time was lightened by laughter.
>
> [. . .]
>
> Our relationship with the Inuit was extremely close. We were friends, collaborators, and, in some cases, mates. . . . We had groups of old women humming, sewing furs together on the floors of our Quonset huts—an abandoned SAC airbase from the early days of the cold war— and the hunters fashioned spears, boats, etc. Much of what we created and did was strange to the younger generation. Prior to our film, many of the young had severed connections with the old ways: they were "modern" in dress (jeans), music (rock and roll), etc. The middle generation had been educated by missionaries to the point that they were in deep denial about much of their past cultural heritage. While the younger people were thrilled to re-create elements of a partially lost

culture, this generation was a bit upset about some of what we proposed to do (sharing of wives, kissing—especially where the two girls put their mouths together and blow on each other's vocal chords, creating the "music" and atmosphere of the "orgy" that followed).

But the much older generation reaffirmed what James Houston had put into his book. And those hunters we brought down from Inuit settlements not yet "compromised" by civilization also were ardent supporters. We showed them pictures, artifacts, testimonies, recordings, etc. Soon everyone came around. And then, of course, they revealed many things to us.

The screenwriters and Kaufman made significant alterations to Houston's rich novel, published in 1971. The most striking is the point of view, which shifts from the book's first-person narrator Avinga to the English-speaking strangers. Whereas Houston's full title is *The White Dawn: An Eskimo Saga,* Kaufman's focus is on the three men. Instead of a voiceover narration—which might have been too much of a literary crutch—the film's images and sounds maintain a visceral immediacy. Unfortunately, Avinga disappears entirely from the story. The son of Chief Sarkak, he calls himself "a bastard, half son, half cripple." Because his legs were deformed by a pack of dogs, he is an outsider to the action he chronicles, from hunting animals to flirting with women. But his marginality makes him a vivid storyteller: he is not only able to blend into the background and see everything but to reflect upon it. For example, he describes with surprise how the three men cooked the fish they caught that day and ate it hot: "We knew how to do this, of course, but we thought it a disgusting way to spoil meat, and the smell and evil greasy smoke that rose from the fish was offensive to us" (103–4). Of course the Eskimos eat their trout raw.

Avinga explains that the camp's luck improves after the arrival of the strangers: once Billy is nursed to recovery, seal meat is theirs in abundance, and a sick woman close to death gets well. But toward the end, the opposite transpires: because the camp's luck is bad, the foreigners are to blame, and they are killed to protect the community. With the exception of Daggett, their effect has indeed been detrimental: Billy (called Pilee in the book) introduces gambling with a contest of precision knife throwing (although he offers Sowniapik his knife in a conciliatory gesture after winning the man's two daughters). Making "moonshine" is not only Billy's idea in the novel: it seems to come from Portagee when he finds in the thawing snow a few buckets of berries they hid months before.

The movie adaptation invents two dramatic incidents to help rationalize the Eskimos' fatal decision. The stealing of the boat has no counterpart in the novel, nor does an Eskimo woman die after drinking the alcoholic brew. (Billy is the one found almost dead in the snow.) Whereas Kaufman presents a more causal relationship among events, Avinga elaborates on the internal tensions in their society: Sarkak is a proud and aging warrior whose relationship with the Shaman includes wariness because each is jealous of the power of the other. In the novel's final chapters, Sarkak has already left the camp (after feeling insulted by the three strangers), and it is the Shaman who turns the community against them. The only ones who do not participate in the murder are the narrator, Neevee, and Sarkak's son Kangiak, who tries to protect Daggett. Disgusted with his own people, Kangiak finally leaves with the American ship whose men come looking for their lost mates. The novel ends symmetrically with the ship's log one year later.

Houston conveys the organic and communal existence of the Eskimo people, who share not only the enormous soft bed dominating each igloo but food, wives, and child rearing. Because the voice is Avinga's, we see the cycles from the inside, tainted neither by embarrassment nor apology. He has an almost Dionysiac understanding of the ritualistic orgy: "It was as though all the people in the dance house had melted into a single quivering animal whose nerves twitched with each beat of the drum" (170). And Avinga expresses a belief in destiny as well as reincarnation. By the end of the novel, he is the only survivor of the community.

In a 1974 interview, Kaufman elaborated on his desire for a more objective presentation of the cultural clash. His alterations of the novel were in the service of understanding "the view of the whalers, who were accustomed to drinking and gambling, but not accustomed to the tradition of the Eskimos lending of a wife to a friend who will be happier after a night with a woman. We wanted to show both the attitude of the Eskimos and that of the others. It was a tragic conflict that could have occurred in a science-fiction story on another planet. The whalers were suddenly introduced into a world of new rituals and morals" (Knickerbocker). Houston knew this world because he lived for twelve years with the Eskimos as a civil administrator. He was one of the first white men to bring Eskimo carvings to the United States; moreover, he also traveled to Japan to learn about making prints and then shared this craft with the Eskimos. He heard the story that anchors *The White Dawn* from relatives of Eskimos who rescued three whalers near the end of the nineteenth century. An amazing coincidence emerged after the casting of Simonie Kiopapik as Sarkak. According to Kaufman, the elderly Eskimo "was standing on the sidelines, and we asked him to play the role. Later we learned that twenty years ago he had saved Houston's life" (Knickerbocker).

When asked what happened to the Inuit since the making of *The White Dawn,* Kaufman replied that the way of life has changed in the area where they shot the film:

> The place was called Frobisher Bay, but I think they've since renamed it. It's about 1,600 miles straight north from Montreal, about four hundred miles above the tree line. Not long before we arrived, the Inuit demanded and won the right to drink alcohol—a victory for equal rights, a disaster for health. Evolution hadn't equipped them physically to be able to process and absorb large quantities of booze, resulting in acute liver problems, violent drunken rages, etc. I saw a number of foul, unpleasant fights. Since seals were increasingly hard to find in the areas around this settlement (around two thousand people), the vitamin content from eating raw seal livers was absent from diets. On top of that, kids (of course) were eating junk food from the Hudson Bay Company, creating terrible dental and nutritional problems. Toss in some T.B. and venereal disease, and you've got the potential for those "frontier" problems that plagued the American West, destroying tribal identities. The Canadian government was trying to respond actively; although I'm not up to date on what's been going on, I have the feeling that they've been proactive in a very positive way. And the younger Inuit were not only involved politically but artistically in trying to shape their modern cultural identity.

Although *The White Dawn* was to premiere at the Cannes Film Festival, Kaufman confided that Paramount decided to send *The Conversation* instead, given that Coppola's previous film, *The Godfather* (1972), had become one of the biggest hits of all time. "*The White Dawn* never really got shown in Europe, and had a small release in the U.S.," he said regretfully. And although he had hoped at the time that more films would be made by the Inuit community, it wasn't until 2001 that *The Fast Runner* brought Eskimo cinema to festivals and theaters.

The Wanderers

Kaufman continued to explore the precarious balance of the individual and the community by writing the screenplay for *The Outlaw Josey Wales* (1976), which he adapted from Forrest Carter's book *Gone to Texas* (after a first draft by Sonia Chernus). "I switched it totally around," he said at the 2001 Philadelphia Weekend Film Festival retrospective of his work. "Forrest Carter was far to the right of George Wallace. I heard it was Abbie Hoffman's favorite movie," Kaufman added. ("Perhaps the last great Western script" is the assessment of the renowned film scholar Tom Gunning [qtd. in Smith, "Auteur!" 39].) Although he was to direct the film as well, creative differences with the star Clint Eastwood resulted in the latter's helming the Western in 1976. Eastwood plays a classic loner—a man of few words and many gunshots—who sets out to avenge the murder of his wife and son by "Redleg" northerners toward the end of the Civil War (bringing us back to the tense time frame just before the action of *The Great Northfield Minnesota Raid*). Although he resists getting close to anyone, Josey teams up with the unlikely ally of an aging Native American (Chief Dan George, who had been a chief in Canada before costarring in *Little Big Man* [dir. Arthur Penn, 1970]). Together with a Navajo woman that Josey rescues, the three outsiders save a group of travelers from Comancheros who are white and Mexican. The pioneers seem to have more to fear from their own race than from Native Americans, the traditional enemy in Westerns. And toward the end, Josey has an easier time making peace with the leader of an Indian tribe than with the Caucasians who have been pursuing him.

On the one hand, Josey is cynical: he leaves a corpse to rot with the line, "Buzzards gotta eat same as worms," while spitting a gob of tobacco on the corpse. (He tends to mark people and animals with nicotine juice.) But he is also a decent man in a violent era, and Kaufman invokes not only the Civil War but post-Vietnam pain. Josey's final line, "I guess we all died a little in that damn war," refers as well to the one in which the United States audience of 1976 had just engaged. Kaufman's ongoing preoccupation with the way things are recorded, mediated, and disseminated can be seen when a shopkeeper has himself photographed alongside three corpses, each set upright against a board. Kaufman's sensibility is equally evident in the script's possibility for community, distinct from the traditional Eastwood image of the solitary hero riding off into the sunset, as in *Pale Rider* (1985). Whether he likes it or not, Josey has created an extended family.

The theme of the adventurer was further elaborated by Kaufman, who created the original story of *Raiders of the Lost Ark* with George Lucas, which Steven Spielberg directed in 1981. (On the occasion of the 1993 Sundance Film Festival retrospective of Kaufman's work, Michael Sragow specified, "Joining the Nazi fascination with occult artifacts to the legendary powers of the ancient Hebrew ark of the covenant, Kaufman contrived the McGuffin for *Raiders of the Lost Ark*" (Sragow, "Adventures," 34). And he spent eight months preparing the script and style of *Star Trek*. Although he was set to direct it in 1976, Paramount determined that there was no market for science fiction. Only a year later—after the success of *Star Wars*—the studio revived the project, with Robert Wise directing.

Instead, Kaufman shot *Invasion of the Body Snatchers* and *The Wanderers* back to back, displaying a remarkable versatility. While both films deal with an individual defining himself within or outside of a community, the genre and style are completely different. In Richard Price's explosive first novel, *The Wanderers* (1974), the director found a surprisingly effective vehicle for his ongoing concerns with racial tensions, sexual stirrings, camaraderie, and betrayal. First recommended by his son Peter, the autobiographical book about the Bronx in 1962 posed a cinematic challenge: while the reviews likened the novel to popular films—*Rolling Stone* called it "the flip side of *American Graffiti*," and the *Los Angeles Free Press* termed it "a kind of teenage *Godfather*" (book jacket)—its interlocking stories, pungent prose, and internal monologues are hardly conducive to movie storytelling. Kaufman and his wife Rose wrote a screenplay that transforms what *Newsweek* called Price's "switchblade prose" into a supple cinematic structure with expressive visual and aural detail. First, they streamlined the collective protagonist—deleting quintessentially "horny" characters like Buddy and Eugene—to focus on Richie and a few other key players of the ensemble piece. Second, they moved the action forward one year: by situating the coming-of-age story in 1963, Philip and Rose Kaufman created a wider sociopolitical context, including the assassination of President John F. Kennedy.

The Wanderers is a delightful, fast-moving period piece that—like *The Great Northfield Minnesota Raid* and *The Outlaw Josey Wales*—reveals the director's affection for rebels in a time of transition. It is anchored and driven by popular songs of the early 1960s. Long before the advent of music videos, Kaufman skillfully juxtaposes visual action with the most effective rhythm, melody, lyrics, and orchestration (especially when we hear Dion's "Wanderer" as the guys strut down the street). He takes his cue from the novel, where a character preparing for his wedding party makes a list of records to be borrowed from each buddy. Under "Richie," for example, is "Runaway"; under "Joey," "Big Girls Don't Cry," "Walk Like a Man," and "The Wanderer" (Price 201). These very songs play a prominent role in the film—establishing the time frame, engendering the pulse of scenes, and evoking nostalgia for those who were American teenagers in the early 1960s.

John Friedrich, Ken Wahl, Tony Ganios, and Jim Youngs in *The Wanderers*. Courtesy of Orion Pictures.

The title refers to an Italian American Bronx gang at a time when white gangs ruled: it includes the handsome, libidinous Richie (Ken Wahl, who went on to star on TV in *Wiseguy*); the hothead Joey (John Friedrich); his muscular protector Perry (Tony Ganios); and Turkey (Alan Rosenberg), who has shaved his head to join a rival gang, the Fordham Baldies. The latter's flavorful members include the hulking Terror (Erland van Lidth) and (new to the film version) his diminutive, big-mouthed girlfriend Pee-Wee (Linda Manz, before her striking performance in *Days of Heaven* [1978]). Racial tensions are foregrounded, especially in a classroom scene that would be echoed in Spike Lee's *Do the Right Thing* (1989): the teacher (Val Avery), in a vain attempt to improve interracial communication, asks the Italians and "the coloreds" to name the epithets they call each other. As he lists them on the blackboard, the students come to blows. The Mafia-style father (Dolph Sweet) of Richie's girlfriend Despie Galasso (Toni Kalem) decides that instead of a rumble, they should take out their aggressions on the football field. The game is broken up by the ultraviolent gang known as the Ducky Boys (an emotionless group reminiscent of the pods of *Invasion of the Body Snatchers*), but these small and silent thugs are ultimately beaten by the alliance of Italian, Asian, and African American gangs. By the film's end, Terror accidentally enlists in the Marines after a drunken binge, Joey and Perry go off to California, and Turkey becomes a victim of the Ducky Boys.

While completely restructuring the novel, *The Wanderers* uses Richie—who opens and closes the book—to begin and end the film. Although he is "going steady" with the gum-chewing Despie, he falls for the classy Nina (Karen Allen) after trying to "cop a feel" in the street (which different characters attempt in the book). When they are found "making out" in his car, he is ostracized by Despie and the Wanderers. But this dissipates in the face of JFK's assassination, which reunites the tearful characters. Richie will marry his now-pregnant girlfriend, and he experiences a wistful moment of acknowledgment when he peers in the window of Folk City at Nina listening to Bob Dylan: the song, appropriately enough, is "The Times, They Are a-Changin,'" and she is clearly in a different world from his. Just as his future father-in-law says that Richie will grow into the large Hawaiian shirt he offers him, the seventeen-year-old is doomed to "grow into" a boring, post-gang Bronx lifestyle.

The Wanderers opens with Kaufman's playful incorporation of voyeurism. Even before we see the characters, we hear "Hello, hello, hello," in the harmony of the Three Stooges. This will turn out to be diegetic sound from the TV that flickers in the background as Richie and Despie are necking. (Shots of cannons firing from *The Three Stooges in Orbit* [1962] provide ironic counterpoint to the seduction.) The fact that we can't see their faces creates a sense of depersonalization. This is appropriate to a film that will explore identity, both individual and communal. The Wanderers know their place as long as they are in their own neighborhood. Once they venture beyond—as when Turkey gets lost—they can't function. Moreover, the tight framing suggests entrapment. Not only can the petting of the couple go only so far, but the enclosed space comments on Richie's chances for mobility. Even when kissing Nina later in the film, Richie is cramped in the back seat of her car. And at the end, unable to enter a nightclub whose music is beyond him, Richie must return to the confinement of life with Despie and her family.

The television screen of the opening returns in the film's most memorable sequence. Richie sees people crying in the street and approaches a store window whose television screens present the shooting of JFK. As we hear the song "Stand by Me," Richie literally stands by his girlfriend in a scene of communal shock and mourning.[17] The assassination of the president (which has no counterpart in the novel) is judiciously placed after the attack on Turkey. He wanders, lost, into a neighborhood that turns out to be that of the Ducky Boys. He is slashed, chased through the dark streets, and pursued till he climbs above the expressionless, violent adolescents: as the sound of drums mounts to a crescendo, he falls. The film thus moves from one death to another—from the immediacy of Turkey's demise to the mediated way Kennedy's murder is absorbed on multiple screens. The bald gang member will quickly be forgotten, while the politician's end will be replayed eternally. As Peter Stack points out, "The film's strongest theme is loss of innocence. The news that John F. Kennedy has been assassinated makes the Bronx suddenly small, vulnerable and changed forever" (D9).

Both sequences exemplify the integration of Michael Chapman's evocative cinematography with a sound track that alternates between dramatic silence and popular songs of the era. Visually expressionistic, the scene of Turkey's pursuit is heightened by a handheld camera as well as dissonant sound. Moreover, the silence of the Ducky Boys is juxtaposed with Turkey shouting, "Terror!"—both the name of the Fordham Baldy who could have saved him and the emotion he is feeling. In the next scene, silence is used as a weapon against Richie at school; the students have banded against his infidelity to Despie. Finally, while the TV screens display the president's shooting, hushed silence is the response.

The rest of *The Wanderers* is propelled by popular songs. When Joey is chased at the beginning, we hear the Surfaris' percussive "Wipe Out." The scene of the gangs staring each other down is accompanied by "Runaway." The parade of female breasts in the street moves to "Ya Ya," while the guys' attempted "elbow-titting" is to the tune of "Big Girls Don't Cry." A different tone is introduced at the bowling alley, where the boys have lost to visitors who turn out to be hustlers: as Despie's father is about to take revenge, his brother chooses from the jukebox Placido Domingo's rendition of "Granada." Each scene has its own identifying music: for example, when Nina plays strip poker with the boys and Despie, the appropriate songs are "You Really Got a Hold on Me" and "Baby, It's You." Despie's anger at Richie's flirting is expressed by "My Boyfriend's Back." We hear the Shirelles' "Solder Boy" when the drunk Fordham Baldies go to a party and "The Halls of Moctezuma" when they leave (about to be enlisted men).

The sequence of the football game also makes vital use of sound: the rollicking "Shout" prepares for the black team's entrance (emerging diegetically from the radio placed on the field by their young mascot), while "Do You Love Me" intensifies our appreciation of their expert moves on the field. Dion's "Runaround Sue" accompanies Richie's entrance into the game, its upbeat rhythm expressing his team's increasing success. Suddenly, the music changes: a sound like a swarm of bees accompanies the appearance of the Ducky Boys. The dissonance associated with their slashing of Turkey returns before the melee on the field, as the gangs unite to fight the intruders. (The fact that all the ethnic groups band together against the Ducky Boys suggests a metaphor for the United States, especially because the Asian American "Wong" gang is more prominent in the film than the novel. Whether referring to the Vietnam War or—more likely—the Korean War, an external enemy unifies the factions within.) The new solidarity among the rival gangs extends to their attendance at Richie's bachelor party.

Montage is an equally expressive tool in *The Wanderers.* If Kaufman uses long takes to sustain tension in some of his dramatic films, the brisk cutting here creates comic counterpoints. For example, the early standoff between the Wanderers and the Fordham Baldies cuts from an extreme close-up of Perry's mouth twirling a toothpick to one of Terror's fleshy lips. And the scene of two couples playing strip poker at Despie's party is a striking montage of reaction shots: as Richie and Joey cheat so that the women are increasingly disrobed, we see the playful Nina; the aroused Richie; the furious Despie; and the overwhelmed Joey. It is not surprising that this visually visceral scene was invented for the film.

The changes from the novel are radical and appropriate to the cinematic medium. Much of the coarse, vulgar dialogue is deleted, and the twelve stories that comprise the book become one fluid narrative. Richie's girlfriend "C" is renamed Despie, and the death of the character "Hang On Sloopy" in chapter 7 is transformed into Turkey's violent end. Gone is Price's second chapter, "The Party," in which the more savvy Lenny arranges for Richie to lose his virginity with a prostitute. Also absent is chapter 4, "The Roof," where C's lethal ten-year-old brother Dougie leads his friend Scottie to jump. Chapter 5, "The Love Song of Buddy Borsalino"—in which he meets Despie—is subsumed into Richie's relationship, as is Eugene's horniness in chapter 7. Whereas the scene of the football game attacked by the Ducky Boys comprises the third chapter, Kaufman wisely places it towards the end of the film, climactically bringing the major characters together. Similarly, the racially charged classroom scene, which comes late in the novel (chapter 9), is better suited to the first third of the film, introducing us to the various groups that comprise life in the Bronx of 1963. And while Price ends his book with "Coda: The Rape"—a frightening incident of Nina being attacked, witnessed by the helpless Eugene—Kaufman ends with Richie's resignation to his future.

On the one hand, Price's omniscient third-person narration occasionally sounds like a camera whirring, as when Richie comes home:

> The dinner table—one bowl mashed potatoes, one bowl broccoli, one plate with four steaks, garlic bread wrapped in silver foil, one bottle Hammer lem'n'lime soda, one bottle Hammer mellow-cream soda, one salad bowl, one jar Seven Seas French Dressing, one unlit candle, one

Richie Gennaro—seventeen, one Randy Gennaro—twelve, one Louis Gennaro—forty-one, one Millie Gennaro—forty-one. In the corner, one television, on channel nine—one Dick Van Dyke. (6–7)

On the other hand, Price's impressionistic details are so pungently metaphorical that they resist concrete visualization. His descriptions of erections are consistently evocative: "She started to cry. He lost his hard-on in degrees like a descending car jack," we hear about Richie (30). When his girlfriend later screams, Richie's erection is conveyed as "shrinking like a speeded-up film of a blooming flower shot in reverse" (35). About Joey Capra, Price writes, "A hook nose and bad posture made him look like a comma" (45). Rather than literalize metaphors into heavy-handed images, Kaufman replaces the vivid language with memorable actors. His casting director was the eighteen-year-old Scott Rudin, who would go on to become one of Hollywood's leading producers. For *The Wanderers*, he and the director assembled a striking group, including Michael Wright in his first film role as Clinton. (Note Richard Price's cameo as the Long Island bowling-alley bankroller.)

Whereas the parents in the novel are pathetic caricatures, Kaufman's adults are more human—for example, Olympia Dukakis as Joey's mother. Price introduces D. H. Lawrence's *Lady Chatterley's Lover* in terms of Richie's father's rant: "I don't want this filth in my house," he says to Richie.

"It's a great book."
"It's filth. Don't talk back."
"Did you read it?"
"I don't read filth." (7)

In the film, it is Nina who carries a copy of the controversial novel, which beckons to Richie when they meet. Kaufman adds references to films as well: for instance, *Battle Cry* is on the marquee at the beginning, and Perry is compared to John Wayne.

The release of *The Wanderers* was problematic, as it followed *The Warriors* (1979)—Walter Hill's far more violent gang movie—leading Warner Brothers executives to fear gang fights in theaters. But *The Wanderers* has become a cult classic, often quoted and emulated. (It precedes *Diner* [1982]—another ethnically specific coming-of-age story about adolescent males—by three years.) Its flawed heroes demonstrate

Kaufman's understanding of the era: "From World War II until about 1963, there was an isolated macho world that guys could operate in." The times were indeed a-changin': Dion was about to be supplanted by Bob Dylan and the Beatles, and 1963 would be the last year of white-gang rule, including that of the real Fordham Baldies.

The Right Stuff

The Right Stuff (1983) is a thrilling and quintessentially American motion picture about pilots conquering space the way cowboys once mastered Western land. Using spacecrafts instead of horses, they stake out new territory. Kaufman not only celebrates their courage but laces the film with irony: the astronauts are glorified—and perhaps exploited—by the media like circus performers. Given the public-relations importance of the space race during the cold war, an awareness of funding hovers in the background of hero creation: "No bucks, no Buck Rogers" is a repeated line (equally true for filmmaking). Kaufman's adaptation of Tom Wolfe's bestselling book is an ambitious ensemble piece (containing over 100 speaking parts) whose center is Chuck Yeager (Sam Shepard): a World War II hero who broke the sound barrier but was passed over by government recruiters for the space program, he was an advisor on the film and plays a small part as the old codger in Pancho's, the bar where test pilots congregate. With marvelous casting (mostly of unknown actors), Kaufman creates an almost musical counterpoint between the solitary Yeager at Edwards Air Force Base in the California desert and the "harmony" constituted by the Project Mercury team of John Glenn (Ed Harris), Gordon Cooper (Dennis Quaid), Alan Shepard (Scott Glenn), Gus Grissom (Fred Ward), Scott Carpenter (Charles Frank), Deke Slayton (Scott Paulin), and Wally Schirra (Lance Henriksen) near Cape Canaveral.

No less sensitive than rugged, *The Right Stuff* keeps a second focus on the wives of these test pilots, women constantly aware that their husbands are as likely to die as to return from their missions. As Stephanie Zacharek wisely perceived in the *New York Times*, "It's the wives who may be the movie's truest heroes . . . relentlessly candid mirrors that reflect their husbands' truest selves—it's through their eyes that we see the men's follies and disappointments, and the tenderest corners of their bruised egos" (27). The director traces the development of camaraderie among both groups; for example, when the astronauts band together against the scientists and government officials who are basically using them, they gather strength.

Although it looks like an expensive epic, Kaufman managed to shoot most of the film in San Francisco for a modest budget. (The fact that the production took precisely nine months suggests a figurative labor of love.) And while computer-generated images did not yet exist, he invented (with the help of the experimental filmmaker Jordan Belson) breathtaking images of flight. Fortunately, its twentieth-anniversary release on DVD in 2003 brought to the film a new generation of enthusiasts.

The DVD extras provide a tremendous amount of information, including three documentaries, fifteen minutes of deleted footage, interviews with three of the original Mercury 7 astronauts—Scott Carpenter, Gordon Cooper, and Wally Schirra—as well as an interactive space-exploration time line with archival NASA footage and a PBS documentary entitled, "John Glenn: American Hero." (Coincidentally, the Glenn documentary of 1998—which reminds us that John Glenn was an Ohio senator and a candidate for the presidency the year *The Right Stuff* was released—is narrated by Timothy Bottoms, who starred in *The White Dawn*.) In addition, the American Film Institute hosted a twentieth-anniversary screening and panel in Los Angeles in 2003, reuniting many of the cast, crew, and surviving astronauts. With abundant nostalgia, the actors recall how effectively Kaufman worked with actors. As Pamela Reed said, "Phil would find you on the set and make you feel like you turned into the child your mother always wanted you to be, and you were in the right place."

The multiple openings of *The Right Stuff* introduce Kaufman's thematic concerns, narrative strategies, and stylistic flourishes. Black-and-white archival footage of test pilots and planes is framed within a square inset. The director makes us aware that his first images are mediated, especially when he inserts Sam Shepard and Levon Helm (who plays Jack Ridley) into this footage a few moments later. As in his other films, Kaufman delights in the interplay not only between the factual and the fabricated but between what can be recorded and what remains unknown: the voiceover says, "They were test pilots, and no one knew their names." The voice is that of Levon Helm, whose first line is evocative: "There was a demon that lived in the air." Although we don't yet know the identity of the "demon"—a shape? the sound barrier? loss of control? the endeavor itself?—it's like the mythological beast that must be slain by a knight. The understated southern drawl constitutes another narrative frame, one that calls back to the verbal source of the film, Tom Wolfe's words.

At the same time, the point-of-view of the test pilots in the plane moves through and around the clouds. This wobbly footage conveys the precariousness of the flight and begins the film's interweaving of natural elements. *The Right Stuff* veers from air to earth, where—a few minutes later—the crash of this plane yanks the film into color. The raging orange flame returns in a few key scenes: it shoots out of the tail of the orange X-1 plane—the challenge that Yeager contemplates in the desert—and later consumes Pancho's bar. Toward the end of the film, the bonfire made by Aborigines in Australia is connected to the "celestial fireflies" that John Glenn sees outside his spacecraft window. Finally, water is used the most ironically of the four elements. For example, when Alan Shepard needs to urinate after numerous delays in takeoff, the intercutting of various liquids is humorous: we see coffee being poured, a hose's emission, a toilet being flushed, and so on.[18] And after Gus Grissom's capsule lands in the water, his floundering in the ocean is the antithesis of heroic behavior. Indeed, bravery is associated with the sky, while Grissom's sweating face conveys panic.

The opening sequence also introduces circular images, which are integral to the film's structure and vision. From a propeller turning to a satellite dish twirling at the sky—recording the plane's speed—this is the imagery of return. Despite the linear thrust enacted by the pilots (Yeager's horizontal and the astronauts' vertical), Kaufman's narrative is rooted in repetition—of flights, orbits, and rituals. Indeed, *The Right Stuff* unfolds more "orbitally" than Yeager's solo flights, suggesting the "theme and variations" approach visible earlier in *The White Dawn* and later in *The Unbearable Lightness of Being*. Kaufman incorporates a dual impulse: Yeager's first and final scenes are about linearity and speed (elements equally important to a motion picture), while the travel of the astronauts throughout the film is seemingly circular and slow. (As the Liaison Man [David Clennon] puts it, nobody cares about how fast they go, only how high.)

This musical structure is inseparable from the film's Oscar-winning score by Bill Conti. It builds organically over the opening title, from the sound of wind and a heartbeat into percussion. Carrying the rhythm of the body into a heightened mechanical repetition, the sound track then introduces the stirring melody, which recurs in key scenes. It is precisely because Kaufman designed such a pervasive sound track that his moments of silence are so potent. At the film's very beginning, for example, the multiple tracks—music, voiceover, and the test pilot's last words—suddenly disappear with the crash. A cut to a sleeping woman abruptly opening her eyes is frightening in its silence. A man in black (Royal Dano) slowly approaches her house in the first of numerous appearances: this minister continues to be present whenever death hovers. He will be seen at Pancho's bar, then during Yeager's testing of the X-1, and even at the spacecraft before Shepard's launch. As the wife of the dead pilot cowers from his news, the silence is broken by the music of an accordion. From a close-up of her face, the sound bridge takes us into the funeral scene. This is not only an economical editing device but a way of expressing what is in her thoughts before the minister even speaks. With dread, she can already hear her husband's funeral.

Kaufman's direction of the burial scene is complex: instead of a focus on the widow, he cuts from a close-up of Glennis (Barbara Hershey) to one of Yeager and then repeats the montage, creating a connection between two characters who don't necessarily know each other. Because her hat covers one eye, Glennis is visually linked to the widow's black veil. Only on second viewing do we realize that the film introduces Yeager's wife in terms of fearing a husband's death. A long shot then presents the air-force tradition of planes flying above the cemetery in "the Missing Man Formation": one plane breaks from the pattern, representing the dead pilot. By beginning *The Right Stuff* with these particular scenes, Kaufman expands his focus from the active men to the wives who wait apprehensively. When the first one wakes up—as if from a nightmare— she not only suggests that the opening (in black-and-white) was a dream but that wives have a premonition of their husbands' fate.

Curiously, the film opens not with triumph but failure, death, and commemoration. Kaufman thus embarks on his redefinition, or retrieval, of heroism. What is the "Right Stuff"? Wolfe's nouns include bravery, "moxie," reflexes, experience, coolness, and ultimately, a "cause" (17). Kaufman makes it clear that not talking about oneself is part of the Right Stuff as well. The first section of the film is a paean to Yeager, whose quiet confidence has a certain modesty. After the funeral, he rides his horse in the desert toward a plane, confronting the orange X-1 ("a bronc that can't be broken," as Kaufman's screenplay puts it). Sam Shepard, resembling the lanky and laconic cowboy embodied by Gary Cooper in films like *The Westerner* (1952), does seem to emerge from the iconography of Westerns. Riding his horse across the vast landscape and then staring at the fire-belching tail of the instrument designed to break the sound barrier, he suggests the rugged, individualist ethos of a man who loves a challenge. Tom Charity's excellent monograph on *The Right Stuff* for the British Film Institute develops the notion that this film emerges from the Western: he calls it a masculine genre—"where white America grapples with its character, its conscience, and its sense of self"—concerned with the construction of the hero, and discusses how *The Right Stuff* is also about pioneer mythology. Calling it "the starkest and most physical of philosophical dramas," he proposes that the Western trades on "fantasies of absolute male autonomy, dexterity, and moral imperative" and sees *The Right Stuff* as a "hip movie about 'square' subjects (astronauts, the military, courage, patriotism)," ranging freely "across apparently contradictory styles: mythic and satiric, documentary and surreal, even epic and underground" (Charity 8).

Chuck Yeager (Sam Shepard) faces the X-1 plane in *The Right Stuff*. Digital frame enlargement.

The image of real heroism is developed at Pancho's, the bar where test pilots congregate under the watchful eye of Pancho Barnes (Kim Stanley). A tough and tough-talking former aviatrix, she exhibits a particular fondness for Yeager and a withering condescension for the young woman trying to flirt with him (played, ironically, by Shepard's then-wife O-Lan Shepard). While the hotshot pilot Slick Goodlin tells government recruiters that the sound barrier can be broken for his fee of $150,000, Yeager's reply is a pleasant surprise to them: he offers to take the risk for nothing. With disdain for money and glory, he goes up to break records because he's after "the demon in the thin air," as Ridley later reminds the denizens of Pancho's. Kaufman juxtaposes Yeager's acceptance of this challenge with a romantic scene that picks up on the eye contact from the funeral. Yeager seems to be attempting a pickup of Glennis at the bar. "Honey, you ever been caught alone in the middle of the desert before?" he asks her. "Never have. Don't think I ever will. Never did see the man who could catch me out there," she responds firmly before walking out—neither one revealing to us that they are married. Yeager follows, pursuing her on horseback, creating a link between the chasing of Glennis and of the demon in the air. Presumably, neither can be mastered and, when he hits a branch and falls off his horse, Kaufman prepares for Yeager's possible defeat in the air as well.

Despite two cracked ribs, Yeager shows up for the flight the next morning, October 14, 1947. We see his camaraderie with Ridley in two memorable moments: to compensate for Yeager's rib-cracked immobility, this engineer fashions him a stick to pull the door shut (and the fact that Levon Helm was the drummer for the Band adds an eye-winking awareness to his twirling the piece of wood); and Yeager asks Ridley to loan him a stick of Beeman's, adding, "Pay you back later." Because he repeats this request for chewing gum each time he goes up on a dangerous mission, the banter between the two friends takes on the glow of a reassuring ritual.

This first flight is presented with visual and aural panache, crosscutting among a variety of perspectives. The shaky images from Yeager's point of view—and the close-up of his eyes behind goggles—are accompanied by a loud engine roar. But with the exterior shots of the plane's rapid movements, we hear a "whoosh" whose loudness is diminished when we see the people waiting on the ground. Again, because of the sound track's layered vitality, the sudden silence when the X-1 disappears is like a sharp intake of breath. (This builds on Wolfe's evocative description of the flight as "thunder without reverberation" [45].) Kaufman heightens the suspense with a shot of the minister—already an emblem of death—and the photos of dead pilots on the wall of Pancho's bar. Sound and cheer return when the X-1 emerges from the sonic boom: the sound barrier has been broken. (Whereas Wolfe tells the reader about the sonic boom beforehand, Kaufman's deletion of the information until Yeager surfaces creates dramatic tension.)

Yeager celebrates with Glennis that night by howling at the moon. Considering that he told her earlier, "I'm half jackrabbit"—after giving Pancho a gift of a snake tail—Yeager is associated with animal imagery. This reminds us that even if his success is defined by machines in the air, he remains grounded in nature. Especially when perched on his horse, he looks every bit the man of the West, and when he later says things like "attagirl" in the cockpit, he treats his plane like a horse. Yeager emerges as the film's existential hero, and not simply because he was a brave pilot during World War II. If—as the influential writings of Albert Camus and Jean-Paul Sartre suggest—a human being is the sum of his or her actions, Yeager is measured by his cumulative skill, daring, and skeptical resistance to the authoritative jargon of politicians as well as scientists.

A cut and change of music introduce the film's second movement, which builds from the loner hero to the group. Gordo Cooper is speeding down the highway in his red convertible, to the consternation of his wife, Trudy (Pamela Reed). The song we hear is, appropriately, "I Got a Rocket in My Pocket," not only foreshadowing the space flight but establishing that we have moved forward six years to the era of rock and roll. Going fast is the bridge from Yeager to Cooper, who zips past a slow-moving truck. But unlike the soft-spoken, self-effacing Yeager, he rhetorically asks his wife, "Who's the best pilot you ever saw?" As he will repeat throughout the film, Cooper answers, "Yer lookin' at him"—with that elastic Dennis Quaid grin that seems to stretch across his entire face. Cocky, gregarious, and competitive, he is one of the new breed of hotshots arriving at Edwards Air Force Base. (The producer Irwin Winkler revealed that this line was added because he mentioned to Kaufman a lunch he had with Cooper; according to Winkler's commentary on the DVD, the astronaut said that he was the best pilot he ever saw.)

At Pancho's, Cooper observes the understated Yeager, even imitating his fingers rapidly shuffling coins. After Scott Crossfield (Scott Wilson) breaks Yeager's speed record—again presented in a black-and-white square inset resembling a newsreel—the scene at Pancho's is charged. Cooper is among the many looking at Yeager to see his response. When Glennis enters, a close-up of Crossfield's glance at her—and of her chilly gaze back—suggest a back story. She goes over to Yeager and asks him to dance, parading their closeness before Crossfield, who can't look away. Yeager returns to the bar and turns his back to Crossfield, who then lifts his beer bottle to Yeager's back. As if sensing it, Yeager (still turned away from Crossfield) raises his glass. Was Glennis once Crossfield's girlfriend? Or does her reserve emanate from a hostile awareness? Now that Crossfield has broken Yeager's record, she knows her husband will return to the skies for another bout.

And return he does, as a brilliant editing moment bridges the bar scene and his takeoff: a close-up of Yeager sipping from his increasingly horizontal glass dissolves to the plane. We are propelled into his flight, which is once again cross-cut with shots of those listening at Pancho's. This time, however, a shot from Yeager's point of view presents a shape that makes him keel over. Is that the demon? Or is the demon loss of control? After this temporary failure, Yeager completes the task, re-maining the fastest pilot in the United States. But a cut to 1957 Russia, where a spacecraft ascends, places the exploits of Yeager, Cooper, and the other future astronauts in a new, politically charged context.

The second hour of *The Right Stuff* moves away from the possibili-ties of a solitary heroism to the team effort required for the "space race" of the cold-war era. Kaufman deftly satirizes politicians, scientists, and reporters at the same time that he traces the creation of the bonds among the Mercury 7 astronauts. Building on Wolfe's often comical tone, he introduces two new and vivid characters, Recruiters 1 and 2 (Jeff Gold-blum and Harry Shearer). The bumbling duo work for the U.S. govern-ment, which is concerned that Sputnik has been successfully launched. As Senator Lyndon B. Johnson (Donald Moffat) flavorfully puts it, "I, for one, do not intend to go to sleep by the light of a Communist moon" (a line that comes much later in the book). The pair present to a group of politicians including him and President Eisenhower humorous footage of possible occupants of the space capsule, including trapeze artists and

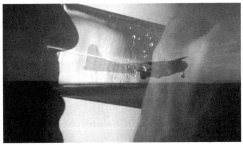

Visual rhymes in
dissolves from a
horizontal glass to
a plane taking off in
The Right Stuff. Digital
frame enlargements.

race-car drivers. Fortunately, Eisenhower insists on test pilots, which
takes *The Right Stuff* back from Washington to Edwards Air Force Base.

Whereas Yeager might seem the ideal choice for the new mission,
he is not the focus of recruitment at Pancho's. Shearer says that Yeager's
lack of a college degree eliminates him. (The fact that the real Chuck

Yeager is standing behind him—offering whiskey—adds a pungent bite to the scene.) Rather, hotshots like Cooper and Grissom are selected, in addition to Alan Shepard. At the moment that "Smilin' Al" lands his plane in mid-ocean, Goldblum and Shearer—true to comic form—are throwing up from the turbulence before greeting him. Kaufman improves on the book by first showing John Glenn on television: he will indeed become the most comfortable with the media, the spokesman and public darling. Here, Ed Harris (looking remarkably like the real Glenn) is inserted into the square black-and-white inset of the program *Name That Tune*. Throughout this section, Yeager remains in the background while we watch the medical tests that the future astronauts undergo in New Mexico in 1959.

The book's early focus is Pete Conrad, who is ultimately not selected for the mission (although he would be part of an Apollo flight to the moon years later). Kaufman deletes this character, instead distributing Conrad's trials among those who will carry the film's narrative. For example, Alan Shepard is the one who must show endurance when a needle is jammed and kept in his hand. Shepard is also the one who elicits the laughs when he is given an enema. Adding to the book, Kaufman prepares for a comic payoff by showing us Shepard's love for—and

The real Chuck Yeager behind Harry Shearer and David Clennon in Pancho's Bar in *The Right Stuff*. Digital frame enlargement.

imitation of—the comedian Bill Dana's "Jose Jimenez" routine on the *Ed Sullivan Show.* A burly Hispanic orderly is not amused by Shepard's calling himself Jose Jimenez with a broad accent. Later, it is this orderly who keeps Shepard from getting rid of his enema. Because the male nurse enacts a comic revenge, Kaufman's transfer of the incident from Conrad to Shepard is very effective.

In one of the film's most memorable scenes, Cooper (again rather than Conrad) is asked by the prim Nurse Murch to provide a sperm sample. After unsuccessfully flirting with her, he takes the vial to the men's room, where the other men are trying behind locked stall doors to do the same. Kaufman creates and sustains the comic tone by juxtaposing a stationary shot of the men's feet beneath the toilet stalls, with the songs they are humming to fulfill the nurse's prescription: "The best results seem to be obtained by fantasization, accompanied by masturbation, followed by ejaculation." We hear bits of the song, "Mr. Sandman, bring me a dream," before the Marine anthem, "Halls of Montezuma," dominates. Cooper's insistent humming of the air-force tune—"Off we go into the wide blue yonder"—with his pants bunched at the ankles provides a humorous emblem of arousal.

Kaufman's cinematic choices are faithful to what he calls Wolfe's "rambunctious prose," in addition to the director's fidelity to the facts. For example, he re-creates the April 9, 1959, press conference in Washington, where the astronauts were introduced to an adoring public in a display of hype. Tantamount to a sly wink, he begins the sequence with the media, a group of hyperactive photographers whose presence is always accompanied by the sound of grating insects. To capture the quality of Wolfe's description,

> A sheet of light hit Gus and the others, and the boiling voices dropped down to a rumble, or a buzz, and then you could make them out. There appeared to be hundreds of them, packed in shank to flank. . . . Some of them had cameras with the most protuberant lenses, and they had a way of squatting and crawling at the same time, like the hunkered-down beggars you saw all over the Far East . . . like a swarm of root weevils which, no matter how much energy they might expend in all directions trying to muscle one another out of the way, keep their craving beaks homed in on the juicy stuff that the whole swarm had sensed—until they were all over them, within inches of their faces in

some cases, poking their mechanical beaks into everything but their belly buttons, (85–87)

he cast the Bologna Brothers, a San Francisco clown troupe that he likened to "commedia dell'arte." Flashbulbs popping, limbs flying, they help create the pedestal destined for America's new heroes. The satiric thrust is maintained when the sequence ends with the "Hallelujah" chorus on the sound track (followed by a cut to Chuck Yeager smirking). Glenn is the only one of the seven who knows how to speak publicly, and he emerges as their spokesman. (That he is the public hero is supported visually: as the actress Veronica Cartwright points out in the DVD commentary, Glenn also wears the lightest-colored suit.)

In a subsequent scene with his wife, Annie (Mary Jo Deschanel), he is established as a private hero, patient with his wife's stutter and cognizant of his own overly wholesome image. The absence of music makes this a quietly powerful scene. Whereas the screenplay has him playing "Amazing Grace" on the trumpet while Annie sings, Kaufman retains only the intimacy of a conversation punctuated by loving gazes.[19] This prepares for what might be the film's apotheosis of heroic behavior. When Annie later refuses to let the publicity-seeking Lyndon Johnson into her home to watch Glenn's takeoff with her—afraid of stammering before the cameras—the NASA chief (John P. Ryan) tries to get her

The media circus greets the astronauts in
The Right Stuff. Digital frame enlargement.

husband to change her mind with a phone call. Instead, Glenn backs Annie up, to the anger of his superiors. While *The Right Stuff* may be essentially about the bravery manifested by "punching a hole in the sky" (to use Glennis's term), here Kaufman suggests that it is no less about the domestic integrity of protecting a loved one on the ground.

Glenn is the only astronaut shown in terms of devotion to a wife, which makes the next sequence more understandable. In Cocoa Beach, the astronauts preparing for takeoff at Cape Canaveral are targets of attractive young women. When two luscious babes enter the bar with the line, "Four down, three to go," and approach Glenn and Carpenter, we realize that they have seduced four of the pilots. A cut to Glenn lecturing the others about keeping their pants on reveals the fissures in their bond, as Shepard refuses to be told what to do in his private life. Grissom finally puts a succinct end to the tension by declaring, "The issue ain't pussy but monkey." They are again unified by the fact that a chimpanzee may be sent into space before them, and, sure enough, the media are seen gyrating around a chimp. The pilots quickly band together against the German-accented—and increasingly exasperated—scientists who show them the capsule in which they will travel to space. Because the press corps is visible in the background—despite their satirical presentation throughout the film—the reporters here become co-conspirators with the future astronauts.

Whereas Wolfe simply says that the men demand changes in general, Kaufman individuates the demands to prepare for each astronaut's experience. Cooper is the one who asks for a window, thus foreshadowing the film's closing line: looking out the window, he says, "Oh, Lord, what a heavenly light." Grissom insists on a hatch, the very part that will define his own landing. Shepard demands that the "capsule" be called a spacecraft, appropriate to the fact that—as the first American in space—he will be seen as an active pilot rather than an "occupant."

The scene of his flight's prelude and reception is deftly rendered. Wolfe informs us that the astronauts voted on which of them would be the first to go up. Kaufman, however, simply extends the mystery, the astronaut masked by his suit. Realism and stylization are blended; on the one hand, the veteran TV broadcaster Eric Sevareid reports from Cape Canaveral; on the other hand, a mechanical clanging sounds like a heightened heartbeat. (Among those applauding the astronaut is the minister from Edwards, who adds an ominous note.) Only when the pilot enters the spacecraft do we see that it is Shepard, who prays "not to fuck up." Transmitted via Cooper to Sevareid, the line is cleaned up to, "Everything is A-OK." Despite delays that force Shepard to urinate in his suit, the flight is a success, and he is seen (in a remarkable sequence that precedes *Zelig* [1983] and *Forrest Gump* [1994]) receiving a medal from President Kennedy. The actor is seamlessly inserted into black-and-white archival footage, paving the way for Kaufman's equally intricate

Kaufman creates the illusion of Alan Shepard (Scott Glenn) receiving a medal from President John F. Kennedy in *The Right Stuff*. Digital frame enlargements.

splicing of performers and Prague street history in the Soviet-invasion scene of *The Unbearable Lightness of Being*.

The next American to ascend to space is Grissom. But his landing in the ocean is far from decorous: because the hatch is blown, the space capsule disappears into the ocean, and he is rescued "like a dead flounder landing on the fish market scales" (according to the script [133]). If the montage of failed rocket ascents suggests a kind of phallic failure, one could say that Grissom's flaw is "premature ejaculation." (As Stephanie Zacharek points out, "Kaufman delights, mischievously, in deflating macho hubris—he treats it as if it were an unwieldy dirigible just begging to have the air pricked out of it" [MT27].) We hear him call heatedly to the rescue-helicopter men, but they try to retrieve the spacecraft first. Ironically, the TV-news version fabricates that he asked the helicopter to save the capsule before him. The media is particularly egregious interrupting the private moment during which his wife (Veronica Cartwright) vents her disappointment at the puny reception he has received compared to Shepard. When asked twenty years later about his approach to Grissom, Kaufman said, "My feeling is, I don't know if Gus blew the hatch or not. We have that long moment where he's trying to get his helmet off. . . . Grissom was a great hot-dog pilot himself, and I hope we could leave a little ambiguity there and see the tragedy of how he and his wife were treated. It had something to do with the growing scrutiny of the public glare that got into this whole world of pilots and how people tried using it for purposes of heroism" (qtd. in Accurso 47). The most extended flight is that of John Glenn. As the November 2003 issue of *Airpower Magazine* devoted to *The Right Stuff* reminds us,

> In contrast to all the Soviet space flights that were only announced after Cosmonauts had returned safely to earth (thus effectively hiding several failed attempts that came beforehand), American missions were broadcast live around the world as the dramatic events unfolded in real time. This contrast in sharing the news of their respective space programs was probably the most telling illustration of the ideological differences between Communism and the Free World. (Accurso 47)[20]

While Kaufman sticks closely to the facts, he also invents a poetic or spiritual frame that deepens the sequence. From Wolfe's mere mention that Cooper is in Australia (over which Glenn will be flying), the film introduces a group of Australian Aborigines. To the sound of the native didgeridoo, the elders create a bonfire and look up at the stars. Similarly, Glenn is exhilarated by the sparks outside his window, "celestial fireflies." Like *The White Dawn*, the film has little Judeo-Christian reference but embraces primitive spirituality through rituals. Since this flight is distinguished by the number of orbits, there is less emphasis on the vertical: we see Glenn and the capsule horizontally, especially in a form cut from a fat cigar that Shepard is lighting on the ground to the spacecraft.

The contrast between the sky and the fire of the Aborigines (blue and orange are complementary colors) is intensified by the sound track, which juxtaposes beeps and dialogue with the didgeridoo. In this manner, we are invited to reflect on the coexistence of ancient or primal elements with technological progress. During his seven orbits, Glenn witnesses (and expresses) great beauty. If the script indicates that he moves "into a miraculous dawn. Music soaring," how appropriate that Kaufman incorporates a melody from *The White Dawn.* The old Eskimo woman's chant is transformed into a symphonic score that expresses Glenn's "wonderment" (to borrow a term from *The Great Northfield Minnesota Raid*) at the universe.[21]

But the orange fire glimpsed in Australia is now in Glenn's capsule. Once he learns that he is in danger because of his nonfunctioning heat shield, his voice hardens. He hums, "Glory, Glory, Hallelujah" during his reentry, which the script presents with much greater detail. But, perhaps because everyone knows that Glenn did survive, Kaufman makes an audacious cut from the dripping fire of the spacecraft's descent to an American flag that is part of the ticker-tape parade in his honor. (The music here is also "Glory, Glory, Hallelujah.") And he shifts more quickly back to Yeager, who seems mesmerized by the discovery of a new plane. This is the F-104, the most sophisticated of flight instruments, and yet another challenge. Wolfe presents this after the Houston Coliseum celebration of the astronauts, but Kaufman makes the two events simultaneous, the montage constantly underscoring the unspoken bonds between the astronauts and their hero.

The camera moves into the darkness of the new plane from Yeager's perspective, and then out of the darkness as we enter the mammoth LBJ barbecue with John and Annie Glenn perched atop a convertible.

This lyrical and connective camera movement is along a horizontal axis into depth, later juxtaposed with Yeager's vertical propulsion. Thousands cheer the astronauts, surrounded by men riding horses, slabs of beef cooking, cheerleaders performing, and Vice President Johnson officiating. The media is there, of course, in full force. They get a bit impatient with Cooper, who unexpectedly rambles in response to their question of who is the best pilot he ever saw. Invoking Edwards Base (and reminding the viewer of Yeager's return), he finally gives them the answer they are waiting for: "Yer lookin' at him." But we're suddenly looking at Yeager, the camera rising up his suited body. His voice is magnified, echoing in the plane hangar, as he asks his buddy if he can borrow a stick of gum. On a subliminal level, Kaufman continues the connection between Cooper and Yeager by showing the latter reflected in Ridley's sunglasses—much like Cooper was framed in the nurse's spectacles. Moreover, the visual tone of the barbecue and Yeager's flight is blue and white.

LBJ's proud introduction of the dancer Sally Rand provides not only a kitschy lyricism but a striking metaphor for Yeager. Because she dances with giant white feathers to Debussy's "Clair de lune" (supposedly nude beneath her "wings"), her movements suggest clouds like the ones through which the pilot soars. Kaufman thus invokes the myth of

Images of flight toward the end of *The Right Stuff* include the re-creation of a performance by the dancer Sally Rand. Digital frame enlargement.

Icarus, who made his wings, flew too high, and fell, burnt by the sun. The ancient human desire to ascend to the heavens—the locus of divinity—is embodied literally in Yeager's taking the F-104 off the ground and figuratively in Rand's dance. Moreover, if the lighting behind her conveys the idea of angels hovering above us, Yeager's counterpoint is that old "demon in the thin air." Has the veteran pilot, with a hubris similar to that of Icarus, merely improved upon the instrument of flight?

Kaufman changes Wolfe's depiction of Yeager's ride by suggesting that he doesn't have clearance; his action is therefore more secret, reckless, and self-contained. (When asked why he deleted the fact that the flight was authorized, the director likened Yeager to the "lone gunfighter going out . . . against authority in a way, doing what he had to do. Even though that wasn't how it happened, Yeager could sanction it as the sort of thing he did from time to time" (telephone interview with the author's class, October 23, 2003). At the same time, Kaufman shows the astronauts exchanging glances of complicity. Amid the hype and hoopla of the Houston barbecue, first Cooper looks at his wife, and Shepard at his (the wives are, after all, part of the "brotherhood" that the film celebrates). But then Glenn and Shepard acknowledge each other, as well as Cooper and Grissom, each astronaut receiving the gaze of both colleague and camera. The screenplay puts it evocatively:

> They all feel it as they look across this place filled with car salesmen and roasting cows, with hunkered-down photographers and swarming pressmen . . . and they know something no one else there knows.
> SAME SCENE—LATER
> In the silence there's the FAINT MUSIC of a long—Pancho's playing, of a time of flyboys and pictures on the wall. (176)

But their additional gaze upward implies their awareness that Yeager is aloft again, followed by a shot of the struggling F-104. As Yeager loses control of the plane, the music disappears, leaving only sound effects. He ejects—the sudden stillness is again breathtaking—and falls silently in space as we return to Rand on the stage. We can still hear his fall when the camera is on the astronauts, yoking the two scenes together. A cut to black smoke billowing (similar to the first crash in *The Right Stuff*) leaves us wondering if Yeager is dead. In Wolfe's version, he is rescued by a helicopter. But Kaufman creates an indelible visual image as Yeager emerges from the flames. Although badly wounded, he walks determinedly towards the truck in which Ridley searches for him, still chewing his wad of gum. The heat mirage makes it seem like he is walking on water, another elemental juxtaposition.

Although Yeager has crashed and the plane is destroyed, there is a sense of triumph in his survival. He may have lost control of the F-104, but not of himself—nor of the Right Stuff. As Stephanie Zacharek wrote, "It's fitting that the sight of Mr. Shepard's Yeager, sooty and bloodied after parachuting out of an aircraft that, characteristically, he pushed too high and too far, is one of the film's last and most enduring images. He strides toward us, and toward the future, chewing on a wad of that Beeman's— a sticky, gunky, and improbably perfect metaphor for true glory" (27).[22] Yeager's rescue could have ended the film, but Kaufman adds Cooper's flight of May 15, 1963. Perhaps some viewers are restless three hours into the film (not unlike the country's attitude toward space travel by that date: "OK, another astronaut going up"). Through the window of his spacecraft, a seagull flies amid the blue, suggesting water even if it is sky. The screenplay includes many lines of dialogue here, which Kaufman wisely pared down to one phrase: "Oh, Lord, what a heavenly light," Cooper

Chuck Yeager (Sam Shepard) survives
a plane crash toward the end of *The Right Stuff.*
Digital frame enlargement.

says. *The Right Stuff* ends on a note of awe as the astronaut begins his twenty-two orbits. The voiceover returns, adding a mythic quality: "The Mercury program was over. Four years later, astronaut Gus Grissom was killed, along with astronauts White and Chaffey, when fire swept through their Apollo capsule," Helm's voice says. "But on that glorious day, in May 1963, Gordo Cooper went higher, farther, and faster than any other American. Twenty-two complete orbits around the world, he was the last American ever to go into space alone. And for a brief moment, Gordo Cooper became the greatest pilot anyone had ever seen." The end credits unfold with his spacecraft against the blue sky.

Four months later, the assassination of President Kennedy would shatter the national confidence inspired by Cooper's orbits. Later, the Vietnam War would erode American pride and unity. *The Right Stuff* captures a particular moment when scientific progress, individual integrity, and hard-won solidarity converged. Ernest Hemingway coined the term "grace under pressure"—which the film illustrates—for the kind of courage that is perhaps a precondition for bravery. Kaufman proposed at the 2001 Philadelphia Weekend Film Festival that heroism is "something you do for others" (the team?), while bravery is "done alone, for yourself." Yeager embodies the latter, an image of modest and consistent endurance. Might it be heroic not to change in a world of technological progress? "Yeager bursts the membrane," Kaufman said, "but maybe never catches that demon. I like the 'bookend' feeling at the end of the film where Gordo says, 'Oh, Lord, what a heavenly light.' And in the middle, John Glenn is surrounded by the mysterious fireflies (and the aborigine vibes). Maybe it's all a mystery, filled with yearnings (songs like 'Faraway Places') and the heroism required to go off into the unknown with that cool '50s leather-jacket-hip-Grace-under-pressure quality."

The changes Kaufman made to Wolfe's book are revealing. Originally a series of four articles written for *Rolling Stone* in 1973, *The Right Stuff* was published in 1979 (and again in 1983, the year of the film's release, as well as 2001). Hailed as a prime example of the New Journalism,[23] the nonfiction novel hardly smacks of cinematic potential. Teeming with characters, incidents, points of view, and contexts, it is tied together by Wolfe's salty prose—a delight in language itself, as one can see from his description of the luscious females who came to Pancho's—"young juicy girls in their twenties with terrific young conformations and sweet cupcakes and loamy loins . . . moist labial piping little birds who had somehow learned that at this strange place in the high Mojave lived the hottest young pilots in the world" (50). The book begins with the film's second scene—the wives of Edwards Air Force Base receiving bad news—and a focus on Pete and Jane Conrad. Kaufman remains true to the book's chronology, but instead of the cumulative incidents typical of reportage, he shapes the material through a cinematic arsenal including visual rhymes, aural harmonies, and a narrative structure that could be summarized as the orbits of theme and variations. And, as Charity suggests, his rapid cutting is a visual correlative to the "amputated language" Wolfe found among the flyers (58). The writer-director also makes a few notable deletions. For example, the book presents the Cocoa Beach bar where the German scientists sing the "Horst Wessel" song (132). If an audience really heard this notoriously anti-Semitic ditty about Jewish blood spurting off the knife, the emphasis would shift too heavily to the former Nazis. That they now sing "Lili Marleen" onscreen keeps them in the background as comic foils to the astronauts. In a larger sense, two aspects of the book that Kaufman could not retain are internal monologue and political context. Wolfe presents, for instance, the hilarious imagined perspective of the chimpanzee going into space (177), as well as the realistic rumination in chapter 10 of Shepard during his flight. Chapter 11 is particularly engrossing, rooted inside Grissom waiting for the helicopter to rescue him, and then inside his wife's fury at the shabby motel, culminating in her forcing him to call the Holiday Inn for a more suitable room. Wolfe's use of the present tense is powerful in depicting Annie Glenn's fears (247) and Yeager's turbulence in the burning F-104 (340–41).

The second half of the book is a reminder that the astronauts were symbols not only of America's cold-war struggle with the Soviet Union but of JFK's own political comeback after the Bay of Pigs (219). As Charity notes, Project Mercury was about salvaging national pride (13). We read that the Berlin Wall is erected, and later that Wally Schirra's easy flight into space coincides with Kennedy seeing photos of Soviet missile bases in Cuba. Wolfe's epilogue takes us past the film's ending to the assassination of Kennedy and the end of the cold war. The tone is one of nostalgia for the era of the "single-combat warrior" that the astronaut represented. Kaufman ends in a far more celebratory way, with the immediacy of

Cooper's sight as he appreciates the "heavenly light." His description of the approach he took in adapting Wolfe's text is evocative:

> It was meant to be an examination of a quality, something called the Right Stuff, elusive, unutterable, ineffable, but pervasive in Tom Wolfe's examination of the beginnings of the space program. The Eskimo sculptors would spend much time staring at a stone waiting for the figure, the shape hidden inside, to "call" to them; then they would carve out the figure that was already there, waiting to emerge. I suppose I sat staring at Wolfe's book, waiting to find a way to "dramatize" his journalism, yet to retain his exuberant, wry eye. I tried to structure the film without worrying about, referring to, or looking for a "genre"; though it's sort of a "Western" at the beginning, and I was trying to carry that lone rider–Gary Cooper figure from the American myth into outer space (where he sees the X-1, the bronc that can't be broken).

Tom Charity's monograph details the rocky production history of *The Right Stuff*, including different studios, director possibilities, and screenwriters. In particular, he traces how William Goldman—fresh from the success of *Butch Cassidy and the Sundance Kid*—was initially hired by the producers Robert Chartoff and Irwin Winkler to write the script. But once Kaufman came on board, the visions clashed. As the director confessed in an email, "Goldman was trying to do something quite different with the story. He really wanted to do a patriotic homage to the astronauts. He created scenes (such as John Glenn pulling some of the guys out of a Mexican whorehouse) that were not in the book, and which perhaps never happened. And he totally left out Chuck Yeager, that is to say, he left out the personification of the Right Stuff. But the only reason I wanted to do the film was to explore that very quality." Instead, Kaufman wrote thirty-five pages of script notes for a "search" film that could be connected to such classics as *The Searchers* (dir. John Ford, 1956). And, as the DVD extras inform us, he completely storyboarded his vision before presenting it to the Ladd Company.

A significant amount of revision continued even between the screenplay and the finished film. Most of the changes are deletions, perhaps continuing Kaufman's metaphor of the Eskimo sculptors carving out the figure "waiting in the stone." Had the film unfolded over five hours rather than three, we would have seen Trudy Cooper having a frightening dream, Crossfield explaining "the demon in the thin air" to a reporter, Nurse Murch stripping and entering a gyrating "Milkshake" machine with an unidentified pilot, Shepard receiving an enema, and the airbrushing of details from *Life* magazine's photos of the astronauts and their wives. Some of these scenes were indeed shot, as the DVD extras reveal: for example, John Glenn addressing Congress after his triumphant welcome is a stirring tribute to his wife.

Kaufman's screenplay is juicier than most scripts, from an allusively playful line like "the Magnificent Seven Brothers and their Seven Brides" (90), to his description of the press as "THE RAVENOUS ANIMAL . . . And THE SOUND IS COMING from THEM—bubble, bubble, toil and trouble, steam and scream in the most excited way" (83). It contains a good deal of information about what the music should be like. If Wolfe originally invoked a "crazy tango" to convey Shepard's gait with an inserted enema for the medical experiment, Kaufman's script describes his walk through the hospital corridor in the same way, and the piece of music we hear in the final film is—with an ironic bite—a tango! Toward the end of *The Right Stuff,* as Yeager walks toward the camera, the screenplay says,

> And there's some MUSIC THAT SAYS . . . SOME MEN . . . SOME THINGS . . . NEVER DIE . . .
> THEY'RE STILL OUT THERE IN THE HIGH DESERT . . .
> HEADED THIS WAY. (177)

Bill Conti's score fulfills this indication with a return to the main musical theme.[24] A variation of this upbeat melody can be found accompanying Yeager's earlier flight. The sweep of these themes expresses Kaufman's assertion that "it's a great story about heroism, and yet there is not a gun in the movie. It's not like you need to get out and start blasting a hundred people to make a guy a hero" (qtd. in Accurso 47). To this end, he cast as Yeager an actor whose image is more deeply connected to art than violence. He called Sam Shepard "the twentieth-century artist as hero," and to cast this laconic cowboy-playwright as the pilot with the highest degree of the Right Stuff, he decreased the number of lines Yeager originally had in the screenplay. (Moreover, the real Yeager is relatively diminutive in height.[25])

Shepard anchors what is essentially an ensemble piece and one of the greatest cinematic examples of a collective protagonist. Roger Ebert was right to point out in his four-star review that "the new American heroes are team players," contrasting them with Yeager: "The cowboy at the beginning of *The Right Stuff* is Chuck Yeager, the legendary lone-wolf test pilot who survived the horrifying death rate among early test pilots (more than sixty were killed in a single month) and did fly the X-1 faster than the speed of sound" (49). Unlike Hollywood's traditional star vehicles, in which the hero—usually male—saves the day, films like *The Right Stuff* acknowledge the insufficiency of the individual and our struggle towards community. "Living in this more collective time, we are trying to redefine the hero," Kaufman said in 1995. "We're so used to believing there's one way to confront things; but in a complex world, there are a lot of ways. It's not so clear that one person can have all forms of heroism" (qtd. in Insdorf, "Team Players," G5). Films with a collective protagonist depict group dynamics rather than the linear tale of a noble male. Tom Wolfe proposed that the 1970s were the "me" decade, and one could add that the 1980s turned into the "me-get-rich" decade. But the film version of *The Right Stuff* looks further back and creates a model that would be emulated by future filmmakers, as in the homage to Kaufman's film at the end of Steven Soderbergh's *Ocean's Eleven* (2001). By the time it was released on DVD twenty years later, the prevalence of ensemble pieces suggested different priorities, celebrating not only independence but interdependence. Kaufman was in a sense rewriting Descartes's famous dictum as "we coexist, therefore I am."

Fallible Perception and Trust

Invasion of the Body Snatchers

Kaufman is hardly the only filmmaker to make use of unreliable narrators, but his cinematic storytelling is deepened by an interrogation of what we trust as viewers. Whether he presents a gradual revelation or a twist in perspective, there is an inherently political component to his narrative strategy of disorientation: because his films often lead us to look more closely and critically at the images surrounding us, we see how easy it is to be duped, and how vigilant a viewer—or a citizen—must remain.

Kaufman's *Invasion of the Body Snatchers* (1978) is a taut and effective contribution to the genre of science fiction. It is less a remake of Don Siegel's 1956 classic than a new take on the original novel by Jack Finney, *The Body Snatchers*. First published in 1954 by *Collier's* magazine in a shorter version, the novel appeared in 1955 in an expanded edition and then again in 1978 as a "revised and updated" work entitled *Invasion of the Body Snatchers*. Working with the screenwriter W. D. Richter, Kaufman moves the action to San Francisco, making a contemporary metropolis as appropriate a backdrop for "pods" as the quiet countryside. Each character is menaced by an alien takeover, the internal transformation into an emotionless physical double.

Gelatinous spores take root in the city, blossoming into flower pods—a kind of fetus large enough to replicate a sleeping person. The first to suspect something amiss is Elizabeth (Brooke Adams), who works for the Department of Health. Her boyfriend Geoffrey (Art Hingle), an egotistical, horny lout, suddenly becomes an even less desirable placid zombie in a suit. She confides in her boss Matthew (Donald Sutherland), who is evidently attracted to her. Then others complain that their spouses are "not the same," leading the rational popular psychiatrist David (Leonard Nimoy) to interpret the trend as "unstable relationships." The only ones we can trust besides Matthew are his flaky friend Jack (Jeff Goldblum) and his wife Nancy (Veronica Cartwright), whose business is mud baths. They are pursued by the emotionless clones, resisting even after Elizabeth falls asleep and is transformed. But by the end, the new society of replicants has triumphed: when Matthew meets the still-human Nancy in the street, we are stunned to hear him emit the alien scream of denouncement.

The films opens with creative sound and imagery that introduce a poetically askance universe. The eerie music and rumbling sound track—which led Pauline Kael to write that the "roar suggests how God might have started the Creation if only He'd had Dolby" ("Pods" 48)—suggest a hellish birth as we see spores rise. The air carries them at first, and rain takes the spores to the ground. This opening is both elemental—air, water, earth (fire is withheld until the film's close)—and organic: there is a rhythmic force at work, as in the movement of swings, followed by a plant swinging in the background of Elizabeth's house, and later a dartboard in Matthew's office. The sense of a pendulum coexists with a precarious feeling, appropriate to the fate of human beings who are unaware of the encroaching pods. The organic aspect is quite different from what Kaufman described to Stephen Farber in 1978: "When I was working on this, I began hearing *Close Encounters* ads saying that people were supposed to be coming in metal ships. And I put a line in *Body Snatchers*, 'Why do we always expect metal ships?' . . . Do they have smelting facilities up there? In our film they are organic matter capable of adapting to the highest form of life on any planet" (Farber 27).

The back-and-forth movement of the creaking swing on which a priest sits (Robert Duvall, in a cameo of ominous portent) can be related to the doubling and use of reflections in *Invasion of the Body Snatchers*. After Elizabeth comes home to Geoffrey, it's their reflections on the window that we see. When Matthew checks the kitchen of a posh restaurant and finds a rat turd, the owner insists that it's a caper; something is rotten in the state of California. At the book party for the pop psychiatrist, behind Jack is a distorting mirror in which he and Matthew are reflected. (Nancy, who will be the sole survivor, is the only character who is never "doubled." She is the one who teaches the others how to blend in with their pursuers by mimicking their robotic walk.) Broken glass is crucial, too, from Matthew's shattered windshield when he emerges from the restaurant, to Geoffrey sweeping up a broken glass (which housed the spore), to Matthew entering Elizabeth's basement by smashing the windows. And, most appropriate to the film, shadows graphically embody the doubling of the characters: for example, the camera follows the silhouette of a man with a hat exiting the mud bath . . . but he has not left. When still-human characters run from the paradoxically placid and rabid mob, the shadows they cast in the dark street look like a painting of Giorgio de Chirico.

In this context, the cinematographer Michael Chapman's use of the zoom shot has great narrative significance because the flattening of space mirrors what is happening to the characters. *Invasion of the Body Snatchers* is visually expressive throughout, from the phone wire in Elizabeth's kitchen—which eerily folds in like a worm—to the distorting angles as Matthew dashes from one public phone to another. And when he crushes the pod of a singing man and that of his dog, he creates a mutant, a canine with human face. The audacious final shot of Matthew's shout of denunciation consists of the camera entering the darkness of his open mouth (as shocking as the opening and closing shot of Kieslowski's *Blind Chance* in 1981).

Pauline Kael was right to point out that Chapman has a special feel for night subjects, as in Scorsese's *Taxi Driver* (1976) ("Pods" 50). There, his cinematography created *neon-realism,* a heightened visual style appropriate to the seamy streets of Manhattan's Times Square. Here, the camera expresses a city in transformation, an urban and nocturnal limbo between a paradoxically heavenly chaos and a peaceful hell. The sound track is equally heightened, packed with sensation and information. When Matthew approaches a Chinese laundry, we hear a distorted chime and drum. The discomfort continues when an unseen vacuum cleaner accompanies Elizabeth crying to him. (Only later does the camera move to reveal a man vacuuming.) In the mud bath, the sound of breathing after the door closes is frightening, as is the percussive double note heard in the background at night in Matthew's home. It becomes louder with the "birth" image, a pink round "head" emerging from what resembles fecal matter.

Consequently, silence becomes a potent counterpoint—for example, when we see the characters' shadows running past Pier 33: after all the screams, the depleted sound track makes us hold our breath. The subsequent escape in a taxi was indeed rooted in sound: as Kaufman told Gavin Smith in *Film Comment,* "[T]hat scene came to me as a sound scene, where police motorcycles are coming on either side of the car and were going to do something. . . . Just the sense of being engulfed by the sound of the police—the staging all came from that" (Smith, "Heroic Acts," 39). When they escape from the taxi, dissonant chords are effective, then juxtaposed with the song "Amazing Grace" on bagpipes from the loading ship (whose distorted rendition accompanies the end of the film). As Columbia University student Dana Ruttenberg pointed out in an unpublished paper, "Supporting the narrative, the lyrics speak of salvation through sound: 'Amazing grace, how sweet the sound / that saved a wretch like me.' In the film, the sound of the boat makes Matthew leave Elizabeth unattended, to see if they could escape with it. Instead of saving them, ironically, the sound brings on their 'snatching.' The lyrics also speak of sight: 'I once was lost, but now I'm found / was blind but now I see.' These words might express Dr. Kibner's view of 'snatching' as salvation, promising a transformation in a better life

Donald Sutherland
and Brooke Adams
in *Invasion of the
Body Snatchers*.
Courtesy of Walrus
and Associates.

form. The new form of living introduces numbness, which ironically is
the opposite of 'seeing,' and closer to blindness" (10).

When Matthew goes into the belly of the beast, where the pods are
created, the heightened breathing on the sound track is not only frightening but again conveys the organic quality of the encroaching menace.
At this point, Matthew is still our locus of trust and sympathy. But when
he too succumbs to the alien force, there is no one to trust. We learn early
on to be wary of the police and affable psychiatrists. And if we assume
that the most quirky and marginal characters might resist—namely, Jack
and Nancy—they prove just as vulnerable. "You'll be born again, into an

untroubled world," says Dr. Kibner, suggesting a truly frightening vision of groups that don't question their surroundings. (Note Kaufman's savvy casting of Leonard Nimoy—best known as the trustworthy Mr. Spock from the popular *Star Trek* TV series.) "He was meant to be the most logical, relaxed, and reasonable of our characters," Kaufman proposed about Kibner. "But he obviously went to sleep somewhere along the way and woke up on the pod side of things. The message of all religions: Awake. But the reality is that people are lulled into sleep and 'poddom' often by the seemingly most 'reasonable' among us. We were thinking of the growing yuppie presence, which evolved into the dot-com boom and which dramatically altered San Francisco forever, changing it from that more relaxed Barbary Coast city of bohemians, beatniks, artists, hippies, outcasts, and searchers into a city of strivers."

This is quite a departure from Finney's novel, set in bucolic Mill Valley, California, and recounted entirely in the first person by Miles Bennell. A twenty-eight-year-old doctor, he first hears about people not behaving like themselves from Becky, to whom he is attracted; but, since both are recently divorced, he resists emotional entanglement. His friend Jack Belicec—a writer far more ordinary than Goldblum's incarnation—brings Miles to his home to see the "unused" body of a man. Jack's wife Theodora helps him demonstrate that because the body does not yet have fingerprints, it is a blank rather than a corpse. Finney offers the evocative visual analogy of a photograph developing when Miles subsequently sees Becky's "pod double": "The image began to reveal itself" (Finney 59). The trusty shrink is Dr. Manfred Kaufman, whose explanation of "mass delusion" convinces neither Miles nor Jack. Miles destroys the four pods waiting for them in his basement, and a "grayish substance" is all that remains. While Jack and Theodora try to drive away from the increasingly robotic townspeople, Miles and Becky—now romantically connected—fight the takeover. In a stunning ploy, with the two pods expectant outside the door, Miles substitutes for their own bodies two human skeletons from his medical closet. The pods replicate this matter, allowing Miles and Becky to then fight their four adversaries with hidden syringes of morphine.

As they flee, they find rows of pods growing and manage to burn most of them with gasoline. Amazingly, the pods ascend into the night sky like receding dots, taking leave of the "inhospitable planet" (212). The book ends with a doctor's intelligent skepticism, as Miles acknowledges how "the human mind exaggerates and deceives itself" at the same time that he asserts the veracity of his tale (216). In this happy ending, not only do all four principal characters survive but Mill Valley revives through new inhabitants. The human beings triumph, banishing the alien substance. Kaufman makes a darker, cautionary tale in which the heroic impulse is insufficient.

The previous film adaptation is also less optimistic than Finney's story. Perhaps because it was made in the aftermath of the McCarthy trials, Don Siegel's *Body Snatchers* (1956) invites a more political interpretation than does Finney's or Kaufman's. Whether one chooses to see the robotic replicants as representing the conformity of Stalinism or of McCarthyism, the film valorizes the individual of conscience. Much like *High Noon* in 1952, its narrative eliminates "supporting" characters until the hero is left alone against the cowardly crowd. Kevin McCarthy stars as Miles, who will end up the only human survivor of the pods. He manages to keep Becky (Dana Wynter) vital till the penultimate sequence, when she succumbs to sleep for only a moment: in a close-up of their kiss, we see from Miles's horror the recognition that the woman in his embrace is no longer real. The downbeat ending leaves him yelling on the highway to indifferent ears. However, the studio imposed a prologue and epilogue that make for a happier ending: Miles's story is believed by a doctor as well as by a representative of the government, and the FBI will be called in to presumably handle the situation.

With a wink at the original, the actor makes a cameo appearance in Kaufman's film: "They're coming!" he yells while darting through traffic, suggesting that the action of the remake follows that of the original film. While rehearsing this scene, according to the director, McCarthy was approached by a near naked homeless man, one of a crowd of bystanders who had been watching the filming. "Wasn't you in the first one?" the homeless man asked. "Yes, I was," the actor responded. The man sneered, "The original was better." Whether the original was in fact better is debatable (and Siegel's cameo as the taxi driver in Kaufman's version gives it an implicit stamp of approval). The man's comment, however, does address the nature of remakes and the basic storyline of both films, in which "originals"—human beings capable of independent thought and feeling—are taken over by pods.

But the sole survivor here turns out to be Nancy (as opposed to Matthew), a secondary female character rather than the hero. Kaufman ends with a chilling scene that occurs much earlier in the book: the expansion of alien power to other cities. If Miles secretly observes the distribution of pods to nearby towns, we see children who have been brought to San Francisco by bus to be transformed. *Invasion of the Body Snatchers* is ultimately a cry for retaining the idiosyncratic quirks that make us unique, able to feel and express. As Pauline Kael notes, its "deliciously paranoid theme" is "trying to hang on to your human individuality while those around you are contentedly turning into vegetables and insisting that you join them. . . . For undiluted pleasure and excitement, it is, I think, the American movie of the year—a new classic" ("Pods" 48).

Kaufman renders the sci-fi genre a rich form for humanist speculation. An "Antiques" sign beside a garbage truck transporting human remains recalls Truffaut's *Fahrenheit 451* (1966), whose fire trucks are equally committed to sapping "subversive" life energy. If red was Truffaut's primary color in his adaptation of Ray Bradbury's story, Columbia graduate film student Ed Smith succinctly proposed in a class discussion, about the dominance of the color green throughout *Invasion*, "photosynthesis as a dark force." Kaufman elaborated that the "nefarious work" of the garbage men "fits in with Ed Smith's observation, but in a rather reverse way. The mechanical sounds of the garbage trucks are the types of sounds that survive to the very end on the sound track. What we took away were all the sounds of nature: no more birds, animals, etc. And while 'photosynthesis as a dark force' might be operative at the beginning—certainly the pods are examples of nature 'gone awry'—by the end of the film, green photosynthesis has been stripped away. Matthew walks along the row of leafless sycamores: green is gone."

On the one hand, the very notion of body snatching—of taking over someone's character—can be a suggestive metaphor for remakes. On the other hand, *Invasion of the Body Snatchers* demonstrates that a remake can be superior to its previous version. In the excellent interview conducted by Stephen Farber for *Film Comment*, Kaufman exhibits the profoundly humanist impulse that enriches his work, proposing that science fiction begins to give us a sense of mortality, "of things beyond us. It talks about things like deep space and cosmic consciousness. The humbling of humanity is important. I don't mean that mankind should be humbled in physical terms, but we need to be reminded that this is a passing time, and we must treat each other decently because we are all in danger of dying in one way or another. So *Body Snatchers* deals, I think, with a sense of fear and a sense of awe. It's very healthy to unsettle people. . . . We must fight to preserve our humanity, because it is in danger of slipping away from us while we sleep" (Farber 27–28).

More than thirty years after the film's release, the possibility of artificially creating life is less fiction than science, given advances in genetic engineering. But a more intriguing reason for the film's lasting relevance might be the Internet, with its capacity for duplication and duplicity. Don't we live in a new electronic reality, anchored in a hard drive that allows for endless replication and able to invent "doubles" of ourselves in cyberspace? When computers are virtual extensions of our bodies, don't many of us resemble pods that click, absorb, and delete in our solitary seats? "Maybe people willingly 'create their own doubles,'" Kaufman responded in 2008. "Maybe the Internet makes the transformation to poddiness more simple. But for me, the horrors the Internet holds are small potatoes compared to the horrors of face-to-face transformation."

Rising Sun

Rising Sun (1993) demonstrates that a pulp novel can be cinematically elaborated into a meditation on the potential duplicity of recorded images. If the focus of Michael Crichton's 1992 bestseller is the Japanese corporate takeover in the United States, Kaufman's film deftly juggles at least four levels: a murder mystery; a satire on American business confronted by Japanese investment; a mentoring relationship in which a feisty detective is paired with a mysterious sage; and an exploration of whether we can believe what we see. The screenplay is credited to Kaufman and Crichton, as well as the latter's partner Michael Backes, a consultant to Apple Computers. But the film seems as deeply connected to Kaufman's previous work—from the fear of being taken over in *Invasion of the Body Snatchers* to the education by a wise master in *Henry and June*—as to the book on which it is based.

In the sleek boardroom of a Los Angeles skyscraper owned by the Japanese firm Nakamoto, Cheryl (Tatjana Patitz), a young American woman, is found dead after kinky sex with an unidentified man; at the same time, the fancy reception of the Nakamoto multinational corporation takes place one floor below. Two LAPD special-liaison detectives are brought in to investigate: the elegant, Japanese-speaking Scotsman John Connor (Sean Connery) seems to have little in common with Web Smith (Wesley Snipes), a volatile, divorced, African American father. But together they unravel the murder mystery, which is revealed and obscured by technology. Connor is given a laser disc that recorded the sexual escapade and strangling in the boardroom. The killer's face is not visible, until they notice a reflection that turns out to be Eddie Takamura (Cary-Hiroyuki Tagawa), Cheryl's rich boyfriend. Case closed? Not quite. Jingo Asakuma (Tia Carrere), a Japanese American computer video expert, shows them how the disc has been doctored: Eddie's face was inserted. Once they retrieve the original tape, they can identify the man who had sex with Cheryl—and grabbed her neck—as Senator Morton (Ray Wise, who played the villain in David Lynch's *Twin Peaks*). When he receives a faxed photo of his face captured by the security camera, he kills himself.

But a replay reveals that Cheryl was alive after Morton left and that another man entered the room to kill her. When Connor plays the tape for Yoshida-san (Mako), the head of Nakomoto, it appears that the murderer is the arrogant yuppie lawyer Richmond (Kevin Anderson), who works for them. Because Richmond falls while fleeing and is fatally engulfed by cement,[26] we cannot be completely certain that he is the killer. On a spectrum from the very American characters (Harvey Keitel as a bigoted cop) to the Japanese, Connor and Jingo occupy a central role: their allegiance is less to a country than to the pursuit of truth. It turns out that they are also romantically involved. Although Web is attracted to Jingo, he realizes that she is the woman he glimpsed when he first went to Connor's place.

The opening sequence of *Rising Sun* is unsettling, beginning with the sound of Japanese *taiko* drums as the camera zooms into red on a black screen. A jarring human yell accompanies images of ants roasting in the sun before being crushed by horses' hooves; a dog carrying a hand; a woman tied up on horseback. The shocking accumulation of stylized images seems to be from a Western, but the camera recedes from a screen in a karaoke club: this "film within a film" turns out to be the background for the song "Don't Fence Me In" being sung by Eddie and four Asian men doing backup. The film is alerting us to remain on our cinematic toes because there is always something we are not seeing beyond the immediate frame. This prepares for the theme of untrustworthy video images, too: as Jingo later asks, "What's wrong with this picture?" The displacement of Cole Porter's music performed by a "yakuza" barbershop quartet is a witty preparation for the juxtaposition of cultures that the film will explore. (If the images seem like they could have come from a film by Kurosawa, we should recall that his *Yojimbo* [1961] is indeed a kind of Western, while his *Seven Samurai* [1954] in turn led to the *The Magnificent Seven* [1960], a Hollywood Western.) The hands of the woman on horseback are bound—perhaps foreshadowing the bondage we see in Cheryl's bed. They are then untied, appropriately enough, when we hear the lyrics, "Set me loose." Moreover, the severed hand in the dog's mouth might prepare for the deformed hand of Jingo.

As the camera moves further back, we realize just how partial our perception has been: in what seemed like a nighttime scene in an Asian city, Cheryl—fed up with Eddie's singing—gets up from the bar and goes out into a brightly lit Los Angeles. As Kaufman said in July 1993, "If Crichton said he was issuing a wake-up call to America (the economic sector) . . . the film is a wake-up call to what Americans need in film-viewing habits" (Insdorf, "*Sun*," 14). A tilt from her red sports car to the top of a skyscraper tower specifies that it is February 9, 6:13 A.M.: as in *Psycho* (1960), the printed detail of time and place accompanies a voyeuristic self-awareness. While Hitchcock's film took us through half-closed blinds into a dark hotel room where a partly undressed woman is in bed with a man, Kaufman shifts the voyeurism from the erotic to the technological—the "surveillance" aspect already depicted in the political scenes of *The Unbearable Lightness of Being*. In the boardroom, the surveillance cameras facilitate espionage during negotiations between the Japanese and American businessmen. From the Nakamoto security room, Tanaka eavesdrops on the Americans from Micro-Con. Speaking Japanese into a tiny headset microphone, he relays their private conversation to the hidden earpiece of Ishihara, who whispers it to Richmond. This ambitious lawyer employed by Nakamoto then goes to the Americans for an "informed" pep talk. The prominent role played by the video screens expands further a few scenes later: on the same corporate table of that boardroom, we will witness not only the sexual embrace of Cheryl and an unidentified man but the surveillance camera recording it. The voyeurism is far from Kaufman's erotic playfulness in *The Unbearable Lightness of Being*; rather, the point of view we share is that of the person who activates the security-camera angle: we see the sexual scene straight on, then from high-angle, and then close-up. We are led to identify with the voyeur who controls the gizmo—in other words, a criminal gaze.

The visual style of *Rising Sun* is a rich elaboration of the film's themes. As in Kaufman's previous work, questioning what we perceive and therefore believe is primary. It is his fourth collaboration with Michael Chapman, who—hardly coincidentally—was the cinematographer of *Invasion of the Body Snatchers*. As Dana Ruttenberg wrote, "The view of the alien—whether from another country or another planet—is much the same: it is another living organism on our planet (Japanese are compared to ants, aliens to plants), slowly and gradually taking over" (8). She also points out how important it is to blend in with the group, as when Connor prepares Web for interrogating the Japanese, or Web instructs his partner on survival tactics in a black neighborhood: "In much the same way, Nancy in *Invasion of the Body Snatchers* explains to Elizabeth and Matthew how to walk among the aliens without being recognized. There is an education for integration, which is achieved by means of mimicking—that is, another form of doubling" (8).

Reflections are integral in this regard, whether we see in Cheryl in a round mirror within another mirror, or a drummer doubled on the surface of the *taiko* drum. To see Cheryl's murder reflected on Jingo's glasses is not simply aesthetically gripping: it also makes us aware of additional "screens" that can be revealing or deceptive. When she isolates pixels in the video image, Jingo can be linked with the protagonists of *Blow-Up* (dir. Michelangelo Antonioni, 1966) and *The Conversation*, each confronted by recorded images that might identify a killer. Like Antonioni and Coppola, Kaufman seems less interested in the "who-dunit" than the "how-see-it." In fact, *Rising Sun* is perhaps more deeply indebted to *Rashomon* (1950): Kurosawa's multiple versions of subjective flashback become variations on recorded memory.

Indeed, he chose Toru Takemitsu, the veteran Japanese composer of such Kurosawa classics as *Ran* (1985), to create his first American score. The unsettling, flute-based music—performed by an all-Japanese orchestra—invokes yet another film in its use of minor fifths when the

In *Rising Sun*, the glasses of Jingo (Tia Carrere)
reflect the projected image of Cheryl's murder.
Digital frame enlargement.

police enter Cheryl's place: *Vertigo* (dir. Alfred Hitchcock, 1958; composed by Bernard Herrmann). In each of these classics, the score organically creates a sense of foreboding. Kaufman even cross-cuts Cheryl's repeated sexual "yes" with shots of the *taiko* drums (reminiscent of Henry first taking Anaïs while Hugo plays conga drums in *Henry and June*). This fragments or disrupts the sustained erotic tension of our gaze. Moreover, we are told about the *taiko*-drum performance at the party that these instruments "ward off evil spirits"—as if the musicians sense the murderer above them in the building.

The score's primal beats feed into the mythic structure of *Rising Sun*, which can be read in terms of Web (from "spider web") getting the call, meeting the Wizard on the way, and—to overcome evil forces—enlisting the Sybil figure. (Cheryl's seductive neighbor can be seen as the Siren.) Jingo's deformed hand ties in with Kaufman's perception that "superiority in sci-fi is the cripple's mental powers" (interview with the author, July 1993). He transforms the more realistic elements of Crichton's novel into haunting scenes that recall the supernatural realm of *Invasion of the Body Snatchers*. Doors slide open and shut (mirrored by wipes between scenes); ghosts are glimpsed on screens; and a flashforward to Web being interrogated four days later (a scene that opens the book) suggests predestination. As Kaufman said in 1993, "In some ways, reflections are spirits: all that is recorded are spirits" (interview with the author, July 1993). The sound track (designed by Alan Splet, who collaborated on many of Kaufman's films) heightens the ghostly aspect: for example, the sound of a woman breathing suggests that Web keeps hearing the murdered Cheryl; moreover, this breath can be heard in the windshield wipers when Web is driving in the rain.

The film's tone and concerns are richer than those of the novel, where Web is a white American named Peter, and Connor is not Scottish. Casting Wesley Snipes incorporates an additional layer of ethnic tension in Los Angeles—which seems particularly appropriate in the immediate aftermath of the Rodney King tapes and the 1992 riots. Kaufman acknowledged, "It seemed that to make *Rising Sun* relevant to America, it had to take into account our own problems with racism. And that led us to casting Wesley. Joe Roth, head of Fox at the time, had worked with Wesley; I flew to Orlando where he was shooting a film and was surprised to discover that he was already something of a student of Japanese culture."[27] And once Sean Connery was cast as Connor, Kaufman added what he called "Scotland 'Back' Yard: It's the first time since the Bond movies that you feel Sean Connery one step ahead of villainy, comfortable with technology, moving with invulnerability . . . back to the man using his unique talents to seek out secrets." In the book, the lab technician Theresa—who deciphers the discs and discovers their contents—is a minor character. The film renders her a complex, wise Japanese American woman. As Columbia student Lisa Tarchak wrote, "Jingo is a teacher, the possessor and translator of knowledge, a huge development from her more subservient and predictable place in the novel. In the film her abilities verge on the mystical; she weaves technology with talk of tradition and ghosts, and because of her skill, she is able to see what others do not" (5–6). Through Jingo, technology paradoxically becomes the bridge to a spiritual world.

The enhancement of Theresa into Jingo exemplifies the film's more positive treatment of the Japanese, which also includes changing the murderer from Ishigura to Richmond. In fact, Kaufman's adaptation adds humor through the cultural gap between American and Japanese characters. Lieutenant Graham (Harvey Keitel) says things like "Geronimo" upon entering the room that includes the corpse and Japanese executives, or—in response to an offer of sushi—"If I get a craving for mercury, I'll eat a thermometer." Connor recognizes respectfully about the Japanese, "We may come from a fragmented, rap MTV culture, but they don't." (Kaufman wrote his undergraduate thesis at the University of Chicago about the internment of Japanese Americans during World War II [Mitchell 60]).

Whereas the book presents the manipulation of video images as a Japanese deception, Kaufman turns the doctoring of footage into a more philosophical and universal issue. Does technology enable duplication without duplicity? If the disc is duped, is the viewer necessarily duped too? Are recorded images faithful reproduction, or merely representation? These questions can be found in Kaufman's other films as well. (Columbia student Nathaniel Bryson's paper proposed that in "both technology and the body snatchers, Kaufman illustrates the perfect vehicles of consumption. Both are indifferent, constantly adapting, and self-sufficient" [10].) They propose that technology is neither inherently good nor evil; the real question is who is manipulating it—whether American or Asian—and whether viewers resist manipulation by being wary skeptics.

Kaufman toys with us by including a TV show in which Senator Morton is among "real" journalists like Michael Kinsley, Eleanor Clift, and Clarence Page. The senator's claim that he will vote against the sale of the American company Micro-Con to the Japanese is broadcast in the boardroom and provides the bridge to Cheryl's apartment, where the same program is on her TV. He is blackmailed by the Japanese—who have the disc of his escapade with Cheryl—into changing his vote. When he realizes that he is implicated in her murder, he yells at Ishihara (Stan Egi), "You said the fucking technology would protect me!" Rather, he is doubly "framed"—by the internal screens of *Rising Sun* as well as the corporate plotting.

This is equally true of Eddie, whose face caught in the surveillance camera's lens makes him a prime suspect. But, as in the opening sequence, nothing is what it seems. When his car crashes and his body is burned beyond recognition, it turns out that the corpse is Tanaka, who was playing both sides. Eddie thwarts our expectation a final time when he gives himself up: a close-up of him looking at Web's vulnerable daughter Zelly suggests that he is sacrificing himself on their behalf.

Sean Connery in front of a monitor's four
images of Cheryl's murder scene in *Rising Sun*.
Digital frame enlargement.

Kaufman makes us more attentive moviegoers, as in the early scene
that *Film Comment*'s Gavin Smith explored with the director: "When
Cheryl is watching the senator on TV and she's smiling slightly," Kaufman said, "we at that point have no idea that it means anything, and why
Eddie is laughing. But those three characters have a relationship that's
going to go through the whole movie, and it's a seminal moment in the
structuring of the film" ("Heroic Acts" 39). We have to watch *Rising Sun*
a second time to appreciate *retroactive reasoning*—a term developed
by Krzysztof Kieslowski and his cinematographer Piotr Sobocinski—or
the significance of details whose meaning becomes apparent only later.
And his addition of rain to Crichton's novel does not simply add a murky
mood; it literally forces us to look more intently at the action.

The film eschews the elements that led to attacks of "Japan bashing"
on the novel, replacing Crichton's pessimistic indictment with an often
playful exploration of codes of honor. Even the opening in a karaoke
club suggests a humorous hybrid—a Japanese presence in the United
States—that is less invasive than delightfully pervasive. Kaufman elaborated that Crichton's novel came to him and his son Peter—a producer
who majored in Asian studies at Berkeley—in manuscript form:

We took it to Fox and developed it into a screenplay before the book was actually released—to a veritable shit-storm of controversy. The book was condemned in some circles as being "Japan bashing"; and was praised in other circles as being very necessary and brave in its approach. I hadn't agreed with some of what was in the book, and we had already made great changes. Not only was Web an African American, but the actual killer was no longer a Japanese strangling a beautiful blonde: the blond Kevin Anderson became the American villain.

Most of the film studios were owned by Japanese corporations at the time. My first day on the Fox lot, I ran into Robin Williams, who pointed at me in front of a crowd, shouting: "Here comes idiot Phil Kaufman, shooting *Rising Sun* for last American studio!" In a way it was a dangerous adventure (mysteriously, it was many years before I worked again): the film was picketed, and bomb threats were made—always by people who hadn't seen the film. I (and Toru and the hundreds of Japanese who worked on the film) felt that we were taking on an important subject. It was easy—almost necessary to gain "credibility"—in those post-Vietnam years to attack the FBI, the CIA, and American policies; but the murky world of globalizing business was seldom dealt with in movies. I felt that in having Sean Connery teach the highest values of Japanese culture to a young African American (the *senpai-kohai* relationship), I was presenting a complimentary view of the Japanese (the *sempai* was teaching the audience as well) and returning some of the finer values Kurosawa and others had given to us.

If *Rising Sun* explores "the shadowland"—the Japan-controlled part of Los Angeles—the next film on which Kaufman worked is a real cross-cultural adventure. He was the executive producer and narrator of *China: The Wild East* (1995), directed by his son, Peter Kaufman. This documentary about transformations in China depicts the turbulent blend of budding capitalism with the ghosts of Mao and the Cultural Revolution. Its curious eye embraces everything from the new sport of "horse basketball" (in which lavishly costumed women excel) to the "forbidden city" that has become the "for-business" city. This Kaufman-family production conveys a sense of excitement, chaos, economic imbalance, and discovery—nouns that could also apply to a filmmaker preparing to make a movie. Philip Kaufman was about to direct *The Alienist* at the time, having adapted the novel by Caleb Carr. But after two years of discovery, economic imbalance, and excitement, the chaos of studio decision-making resulted in the halting of the project.

Twisted

"Photos never lie," says John Mills (Samuel L. Jackson), the apparently upright San Francisco police commissioner in Kaufman's twelfth feature. But photographs prove to be just as duplicitous in *Twisted* (2004) as the video images in *Rising Sun*. At the very least, they lie by omission: a repeatedly shown photo of the heroine's dead father—who supposedly killed himself after murdering his wife—leaves out the real killer. Kaufman elaborates on the questioning of perception that was so central to *Invasion of the Body Snatchers* and *Rising Sun*: Can we believe our eyes? Can we trust the person we touch? While *Twisted* is the most commercial and perhaps least substantive of Kaufman's recent films, his decision to direct this studio movie—after initially turning the project down—is understandable. His other efforts were stalled, including a Louis Armstrong film; Saul Bellow's *Henderson the Rain King*; and *Liberace* with Robin Williams. Ashley Judd sought him out, and the Paramount studio head Sherry Lansing convinced him to commit to Sarah Thorp's script (which Kaufman then rewrote, although he did not receive WGA credit). Thematically, *Twisted* continues his concern with female sexuality, identity doubling, and the untrustworthy nature of what is recorded.

Jessica (Judd) is a smart, tough San Francisco cop who is promoted to homicide-division inspector by the commissioner (Jackson). John raised Jessica after her father—also a policeman, and his partner—killed her mother and himself. At least that's the official version, confirmed by the police psychologist (David Strathairn) when she claims that her personal life has nothing to do with her profession. Jessica habitually picks up handsome strangers in a bar, engages in rough sex, and forgets about them. Her nocturnal ritual ends with drinking Cabernet Sauvignon in her apartment and then blacking out. When she awakens to a call from her new partner Mike (Andy Garcia), her first case in homicide is uncomfortably personal: the victim turns out to be a former one-night stand. After her second blackout, she is called to the scene of another murder; a tattoo of two musical notes on the corpse's hand leads Jessica and the audience to realize that the victim is the man she picked up a few scenes earlier. (And a cigarette burn on the hand of both men suggests the signature of a serial killer.) Because we do not see what transpires during Jessica's blackouts, her point of view is no longer trustworthy. And if her father was a killer, might this instinct be in her blood too? She certainly seems full of rage, often expressed violently: she kicks her first assailant in the face after he is handcuffed; attacks a cop who insults her; and pummels the face of an ex-boyfriend she finds waiting in her apartment. But what turns out to be in her blood is literal rather than metaphorical, namely Rohipnol (the "date-rape drug"), which makes her lose consciousness. We realize this only after she gives her blood sample to the lab technician, Lisa (Camryn Mannheim), fearing it might match the DNA found on the corpse. At this point, we assume the killer is really Mike, who followed her when she picked up the guy with musical notes on his hand. But Jessica sees that Mills drugs Mike and plants evidence in his home. During the film's nocturnal climax on the murky waterfront, Jessica confronts and kills the serial murderer: the police commissioner.

What might have been merely a formulaic thriller is enriched by Kaufman's cinematic storytelling. The opening of *Twisted* unfolds like a visual echo of the first shots of *Quills*, a slow reveal that begins sensuously and ends violently. With the sound of wind and birds, a black screen opens to the clouds of San Francisco. Aerial exterior shots of the Golden Gate Bridge in the fog are disquieting; as Columbia student Davide Fabbian wrote in an unpublished paper, the bridge "looks almost suspended in the cloud, appearing to be a place of mystery and deception. In the Bay Area, the earth and the ocean meet, and depart, reaching up into hills and peaks, creating drastic angles that increase a sense of unease and oddness. These natural obstacles prevent clear human perception, increasing the fear of what the fog might conceal" (8). The sense of place—and of mystery—is heightened by shots of sea lions, animals that live between land and water. Amid these elemental images, the sudden close-up of an eye is disconcerting. Flying birds are then reflected in that eye before a drop of liquid (a tear? sweat? semen?) descends the female face, bringing us to the fuller shot of Jessica. A man grips her from behind. As in Kaufman's previous film, the woman who seems to be in an erotic embrace turns out to be menaced by a man with a weapon. Here, the assailant has a knife poised under Jessica's ear. (Later, when she looks at crime photos of her family, an X marks the same point under the ear of her mother.)

As in *Invasion of the Body Snatchers*, liquid adheres to the skin's surface in an ominous way, especially in light of the blood about to spurt from her neck. And the density of the air is reminiscent of Prague's oppressive mist in the later scenes of *Unbearable Lightness*. Because of the camera's tight framing, no figure-ground relationship is established: she could be lying down. But when she breaks the armed man's grip and attacks him, it is clear that Jessica stands tall. Although she seemed to be a damsel in distress, she is violent rather than vulnerable. In his DVD commentary, Kaufman aptly calls the opening sequence a "prologue," that introduces motifs that will be repeated and amplified. For example, Jessica wields more than a gun: when she calls her partner for backup, the speed dial on her cell phone is a weapon too, one that will prove crucial in the film's last scene; it is a recording device that can be connected to Kaufman's exploration of surveillance. The director's use of a musical term reminds us that Mark Isham's fine, moody score is integral to the film's "noir" tone, especially Isham's trademark muted trumpet (also haunting in movies from Alan Rudolph's *Choose Me* [1984] and *The Moderns* [1988] to Robert Altman's *Short Cuts* [1993]).

Point of view is in question throughout the film. If *Twisted* is from the perspective of the heroine, we quickly realize that she is not a trust-

At the end of *Twisted*, Ashley Judd
holds up her two weapons: gun and cell phone.
Digital frame enlargement.

worthy narrator. Shots that are not from her vantage point leave out the subject, creating ambiguity. For example, when she has sex with the first man she picks up, the camera is outside her window, suggesting that someone is watching them. This not only makes her vulnerable but proves unsettling for the viewer, who cannot identify the source of the point of view.

In this first sequence, San Francisco is twisted too. As in *Invasion of the Body Snatchers*, also set in Kaufman's adopted city, the protagonist seems to be taken over by something, to the extent that she questions her own identity . . . as a potential killer. San Francisco exerts a dark force—for example, when Mike points out the bay's hidden recesses of drugs and corpses. Like the sea lions, he lives on the waterfront, where both of the first murder victims are discovered. And, like the resisters of *Invasion of the Body Snatchers*, Mike manages to escape even though he is drugged. (The uncredited cameo of Veronica Cartwright—who played the sole human survivor of *Invasion*—adds to the kinship between the two films.) San Francisco continues to be a ripe cinematic backdrop for the twisting of perspective and identity. Indeed, Jessica's blackouts can be likened to the fearful sleeping moments of *Invasion*: losing consciousness leads to being consumed by something that cannot be controlled. (One can also connect *Twisted* to *The Conversation*, which is set in San Francisco as well. Given the technological boom that has taken place in this city, the Barbary Coast is an appropriate locale to question technological perception—whether it's Coppola's portrait of the surveillance expert played by Gene Hackman, or Kaufman's cop who doesn't know that she is being followed and perhaps framed.) Davide Fabbian points out that the protagonists of both *Twisted* and *Invasion of the Body Snatchers* have a view from their back deck directly on the Transamerica Building, the San Francisco icon where the pods begin their invasion: "Besides standing as the tallest and most modern building in the city, it is a notorious point of surveillance. There are four cameras pointed in the four cardinal directions at the top of the building, and four screens in the lobby that allow visitors to control the direction and zoom of the cameras" (5).

The title's literal meaning is invoked when John says that her father's excessive love for her mother "twisted" him. But the facts have been twisted by John, who was in love with Jessica's mother: he killed this woman for her alleged promiscuity. Jessica realizes this only when John takes out his handkerchief to wash away the incriminating evidence of the Rohipnol that he has placed in Mike's wine. Moreover, she wraps her own finger—after pricking it for a blood sample—in a white handkerchief. Kaufman thus invokes *Othello* and suggests that John has been an Iago figure. (In the DVD commentary, the director mentions that Samuel L. Jackson sought this role, which was not written for an African American.) His identity has been twisted as well, from one who pursues criminals to a killer himself. The film is enriched by John's image as a "director." He stages and manipulates. He frequently asks Jessica what she sees, not only testing the perceptual skills that make her a good cop but reflecting what Kaufman's films ask of the viewer. He is a Svengali figure—much like the *kohai* to the *sempai* of *Rising Sun*—attempting to mold Jessica into a double of himself. His desire seems less sexual than psychological, turning her into a real partner who will be complicit in his secrets. In terms of the "rite of passage" theme of *Twisted,* he forces her in the last scene to engage in her final test—to kill, even if he is the object of her gunshot.

The title is perhaps most resonant in terms of what the film does with clichés: unlike Hollywood movies that culminate in the hero saving the damsel in distress, at the end of *Twisted,* the female cop protects the incapacitated male. The film transcends the stereotype that exists both in John's mind and Hollywood tradition—that a woman must be punished (usually killed) for her promiscuity. Given the film-noir tone of *Twisted,* it is apt that Kaufman compared Judd to Barbara Stanwyck in interviews. But with her short hair, leather jacket, pants, and boyish as opposed to voluptuous figure, the androgynous Judd is lean and mean, agile rather than fragile.

The movie that *Twisted* evokes most deftly is *Touch of Evil:* Orson Welles's 1959 classic ends with the corrupt cop (Welles) falling into the water and dying. He has been revealed as guilty by a tape recording. The police officer holding the tape recorder (Charlton Heston) is Hispanic, and—like Andy Garcia's character in *Twisted*—must overcome the false evidence that the lying cop has planted in the apartment of an innocent man. Here, it is Jessica's cell phone that functions as a recording device in the final scene: when she hits the speed-dial button, she secretly broadcasts John's damaging confession. Sound is a crucial narrative element throughout Kaufman's film, particularly the click of a cigarette lighter that we hear during Jessica's blackouts. (Note that Mike lights his cigarettes with matches, whereas the click is first heard when John lights a cigar. We later realize from the crime photo that the lighter was her father's.) It rhymes with the psychologist clicking his pen, which adds tension to his sudden appearance in an empty garage after she finds rats under her car. And the click is poetically yoked to the sound of castanets when she takes a class in flamenco (which connects her to Anaïs in *Henry and June*).

Linda Mizejewski's article, "Dressed to Kill: Postfeminist Noir," pungently connects Jessica to another "female dick" of 2004: Angelina Jolie's investigator in *Taking Lives*. "Both *Twisted* and *Taking Lives* are posited on a 1970s equity-feminist assumption," she writes, "the unquestioned expertise of a woman in a male profession—not a profession like law, in which women are now present in considerable numbers—but police work, the dirtier, more physical side of law and order, in which women are still a minority of roughly 10 percent. This minority presence was made possible only through second-wave feminism and Title XII, the 1972 equal-opportunity mandate that brought women into local and federal police work. These films bank that feminist history into an invisible account, instead foregrounding Hollywood's own investments in the narrative of the exceptional woman, the stardom of these particular actresses, and the recent television history of the woman investigator" (123).

Twisted, more than *Taking Lives*, foregrounds the chilling possibility of doubling: it is not simply that the police commissioner is the murderer, or that the female cop fears she might be a killer. In addition to John's attempt to turn Jess into his likeness, the assailant of the first scene gets under her skin by claiming, "I know you. You are me." Recognizing her violence—a sanctioned rage because she is a cop—he pierces her with this taunt. The film-noir hero and the femme fatale are thus twisted into one character.

An "I" for an Eye

The sum of cinematic decisions made by Kaufman develops an "I" (an identity) from an eye—the inherently visual components of cinematic storytelling. For example, the self-consciousness of a manipulated image—what could be called *fauxtography*—acknowledges that it can also be manipulative: to be aware is to assume a wary or skeptically active relationship to the image. This is what Philip Kaufman asks of his audience—an invitation that contributes to his personal stamp as a filmmaker—whether his focus is erotic freedom, artistic expression, male codes of honor, or twisted perception.

Nevertheless, a coherence of vision does not always constitute the auteurist mark that leads to recognition of a director's oeuvre. Must a consummate filmmaker's body of work be recognizable? Even if we can make a case for the coherence of Kaufman's films, why should this be a higher standard of value than the greatness of an individual movie? Over the past fifty years, the auteurist approach to film criticism has become entrenched, elevating the appreciation of repetitions within a director's work. It is abundantly clear, however, that even a gifted director cannot make a masterpiece without a terrific screenplay. And the contributions of cinematographers, editors, producers, production designers, composers, or actors are often the reasons why a motion picture achieves classic status.

Ultimately, Kaufman is also part of a tradition that has been neglected: namely, directors better known as craftsmen than auteurs. Film studies has perhaps done a disservice to directors like William Wyler (*The Best Years of Our Lives, The Heiress*), Fred Zinneman (*High Noon, A Man for All Seasons*), George Stevens (*Shane, Giant*), Arthur Penn (*The Miracle Worker, Bonnie and Clyde*), Alan J. Pakula (*Klute, All the President's Men*), Sydney Pollack (*Tootsie, Out of Africa*), and Peter Weir (*The Truman Show, Master and Commander*) precisely because of their versatility. In evaluating the work of such artisans, we see not only that particular motion pictures they directed are masterpieces but that each career constitutes a whole greater than the sum of its parts. Even if it were not possible to connect Philip Kaufman's motion pictures via thematic and stylistic consistencies, they would still be worthy of study.

Notes

1. The editor was Adolfas Mekas, who, together with his brother Jonas, was central to the experimental "underground" film movement of the early 1960s.

2. "Monique van Vooren bursts into song on occasion, a sort of homage to those almost comic-book moments in '40s and '50s films where Bacall, Rita

Hayworth, etc. had their seemingly compulsory chanteuse scenes," Kaufman explained in the March 2005 letter.

3. In the same letter, Kaufman wrote, "It just dawned on me that Frank's first flight might be somewhat similar to Yeager's breaking the sound barrier, including the joyous spin at the end."

4. Colette Lindroth perceived that "they are not the sighs and gasps of sexual pleasure, however, though that is what they sound like (and the notion of so many rooms with so many beds suggests a bordello). These are the gasps of pain and effort, and the rooms are scenes of physical therapy rather than physical pleasure" (230). This scene informs her understanding of Kaufman's contrasts: "Like Kundera, Kaufman structures his fiction around polar opposites: sickness/vitality, fidelity/infidelity, freedom/imprisonment, ugliness/beauty; above all, around the opposition of lightness/heaviness. Wisely, Kaufman moves to capture abstractions like ideas and authorial attitude by making rich use of the novel's real and implied symbols" (230).

5. Kaufman wrote in October 2005, "One area that we shot that I regretted losing was Tereza's arrival in Prague: getting off the train with her huge suitcase; then struggling down a huge flight of stairs with the suitcase, falling and sliding down in a great clown act worthy of Buster Keaton (as a child she had studied to be a clown with the Fratellinis). . . . Binoche was amazing: not enough of her clown side has been revealed in her films. But we decided to stick with the Tomas story at this point . . . alas."

6. Kaufman acknowledged in an email of February 21, 2005, about casting the son (and lookalike) of Luis Buñuel, "I thought having Buñuel kiss her on the lips was some sort of message sent to the departed master."

7. A brief shot of the dance teacher (Feodor Atkin) glancing at Eduardo, and of Eduardo looking back, suggests a homosexual flirtation. This is picked up just before Anaïs seduces Eduardo in the nightclub: a knowing look is exchanged between him and a waiter at the bar. Eduardo later warns her to beware of abnormal pleasures because they spoil the normal ones.

8. One of the film's three editors was the renowned Dede Allen, whose filmography includes *Bonnie and Clyde, Dog Day Afternoon,* and *Reds.* Kaufman mentioned that she cut some of the major scenes, including the art students' ball.

9. James Greenberg cleverly calls attention to how Sade's increasingly desperate attempts at writing give "new meaning to putting your body on the line for your art" (55).

10. An intriguing visual resemblance to the paintings of Lucian Freud was proposed by Ophra Yerushalmi, a pianist who sat in on my class devoted to *Quills:* Kaufman responded in an email of February 2002, "I love Lucian Freud. Geoffrey naked certainly has some of the 'lived in' lines of his major models. Let's look on him more as a mere 'Freudian slip' of a figure."

11. At the Philadelphia Weekend Film Festival on February 24–25, 2001, Kaufman also invoked the primordial folk myth of two young people "living in

the Garden: the Abbé and Madeleine are in this 'asylum'—a curative world with harmonies—where even pornography can exist. The serpent whispers in the ear of Rush, and they are banished from the Garden. 'You will learn the knowledge of good and the knowledge of evil.' Too often, all we're concerned with is the knowledge of nice, and we tend to lose our way. Sade in fact is a monster, and art can be dangerous. But things he said led to Simone de Beauvoir or Angela Carter or Camille Paglia—who has put the Marquis at the center of her sexual identity—or Octavio Paz, or Luis Buñuel. And Sade was certainly a precursor of Nietzsche."

12. Kaufman added that the costume designer Jacqueline West, "ever the complete scholar," studied Delacroix's painting "L'Orpheline": "This was the period of her art history major at Berkeley," he said, praising "her plan and overview of the costumes the different characters wore."

13. Mme. Leclerc's presence adds to the film a layer that Lauren Schwartz interprets perceptively. When Madeleine transcribes the story that the Marquis penned in red wine on his sheets, her blind mother asks her to read it aloud. Reluctantly, Madeleine complies: "Monsieur Bouloine was a man whose erotic appetites might be discreetly described as . . . post-mortem. A habitué of cemeteries, his proudest conquest was a maid six decades his senior, deceased a dozen years." Schwartz describes how "the mother feigns shock . . . 'Oh that's terrible! . . . ' Madeleine looks exasperated, as if she should have known better than to read this disgusting prose to her old mum. Then the older woman surprises us all: 'Well . . . go on!' Madeleine grins slowly, and leans in toward her mother conspiratorially. It is almost as though in that brief moment, she has experienced her mother's company in a new way. The two are suddenly old girlfriends, sharing an outrageously scandalous story over a cup of tea on a cold night." They laugh outrageously when the story ends, leading Schwartz to propose that "this brief exchange is among the most memorable moments in *Quills* . . . depicting an older woman enjoying a raunchy story with her grown daughter. While it sounds distasteful and crude, the incident couldn't be more endearing. Onscreen, Winslet and Whitelaw play the beats perfectly, and what emerges is a sympathetic treatment of a subject that is perhaps more taboo than Sade's writing itself: its enjoyment by two otherwise wholesome and completely well-adjusted women. They are neither depraved nor perverted, but are comfortable enough . . . to enjoy a story depicting a sexual exploit so completely over-the-top that it can only be laughed at" (26–27).

14. Wright also said, "Sade's stuff has been around for two hundred years, and we can still smell its stink" (qtd. in Chute 79).

15. It is possible that Benoit Jacquot took even greater liberties with historical fact than Kaufman: the French director acknowledged, after a preview screening of *Sade* on April 17, 2001, at New York's Lincoln Center, that the film's events are all fiction.

16. The cinematographer was Bruce Surtees, whose credits include more traditional Westerns like *The Shootist* and *Pale Rider*, as well as a contemporary

canvas of films such as *Lenny, Risky Business, Beverly Hills Cop,* and *Dirty Harry.*

17. The scene prefigures the moment in *The Unbearable Lightness of Being* after Tereza confronts Tomas about his infidelity: personal betrayal is subsumed by the nation's tragedy when they find Soviet tanks approaching their building.

18. The juxtaposition of elements is present in the book: Wolfe describes the X-1 in terms of liquid oxygen (42).

19. Kaufman gave me a copy of the (unpublished) Warner Brothers "final draft" of his screenplay, along with the first and last ten pages of the subsequent continuity script. Numerous changes were indeed made to the final script.

20. Given that Gus Grissom was later killed when his Apollo capsule was consumed by flames, it is also possible that he blew the hatch because he had a premonition of death.

21. The Inuit chant imitates seagulls, according to Tom Charity (90). He also mentions NASA's conclusion that the "fireflies" were ice crystals!

22. In the telephone interview with my students, Kaufman added that Beeman's and Yeager were "great old flavors . . . two artifacts, in a way, in danger of being forgotten in America."

23. Wolfe characterized New Journalism as the possibility "to write accurate non-fiction with techniques usually associated with novels and short stories . . . to use any literary device, from the traditional dialogism of the essay to stream-of-consciousness, and to use many different kinds simultaneously" (qtd. in Charity 17).

24. Conti's achievement is all the more remarkable given that he was a last-minute replacement for John Barry.

25. In the telephone interview with my class, Kaufman confessed the ultimate irony: Sam Shepard refused to fly.

26. Richmond's death is reminiscent of Turkey's fall in *The Wanderers.* Another detail that connects the two films is the actor playing Eddie's bodyguard: Tony Ganios also played Perry in *The Wanderers.*

27. As Columbia student Catherine Chung wrote in an unpublished manuscript, Snipes's character is "a double outsider: he identifies neither with the white Americans nor the 'foreign' Japanese. He is, rather, a different kind of foreigner, one who is a stranger in his own country" (4). We can add that Jingo's mention of her father being a black American soldier suggests how she too was an outsider in her native Japan.

Interview with Philip Kaufman |

From the author's onstage interview with Kaufman at the 92nd Street Y in Manhattan, December 9, 1993. (Additional portions are drawn from the author's email correspondence with Kaufman and a letter of March 2, 2001.)

ANNETTE INSDORF: In an early scene of *Invasion of the Body Snatchers*, Donald Sutherland's character finds a rat turd in an elegant French restaurant, and you get the sense that something is rotten in the state of California. This was 1977–78, and you took the 1956 images of conformism, making them all too appropriate for the pre-Reagan era and yuppie society. When you made the film, did you feel the timing was right for another *Invasion*?

PHILIP KAUFMAN: That's really why we made it. We felt that theme needed restating. We originally started out to make it in a small town, as we were going for a much truer remake of Don Siegel's original. But then it dawned on us that the place for conformity in the '70s—and ever since the '50s—had been the big cities, the places where you were encountering paranoia. When the original was being made, small towns were in a state of flux. If my memory serves me correctly, Jonestown happened just after this film was released, and a lot of the people were coming from San Francisco. So there was in the air a kind of a strange conformity in the guise of a modern, updated jargon. And that led us to the Leonard Nimoy character: as with many of the characters, it's hard to tell exactly when they're a pod and when they're changed. Brooke Adams's husband, for example, who's watching the Warriors basketball game at the beginning, is sort of a pod to begin with; but when he's changed, we sort of miss that old "lump." When he's invested with a sense of purpose, it's the beginning of the terror. Conformity is one thing, but conformity with a purpose is something scarier.

AI: This film is richly layered, visually and aurally. Could you talk about how you worked with the cinematographer Michael Chapman, who also shot *The Wanderers* as well as *Taxi Driver*?

PK: I first met Michael Chapman in Canada. I was going up to shoot *The White Dawn*. He had been Gordon Willis's camera operator up to that point. We just liked each other. So, we went up to the Arctic together and lived with the Eskimos and made that film. We were trying to find a film-noir equivalent in color, which is in some ways impossible. The wonderful thing about black and white is the way your eyes can be drawn with lighting and shadowing. With color, it's just a big feast for your eyes. We spent a lot of time looking at black-and-white archives, trying to arrive at a style in color that gave us some sense of the shadows and the angles of older films.

But we also decided—even though it's a serious subject, of course—to not take it that seriously. One of the problems with sci-fi and horror is the total seriousness with which they're made—especially for a film like this, which has something to do with what is a human value. What are the human values? Somewhere in that list humor should be included, and it hardly ever is, except for in-group jokes or outright gags in horror movies. So we had fun just with our angles: we had our pod angles and lighting, and right from the beginning everything was kind of coded. Chapman and I would be able to say, "Okay, this guy is a pod already. So, he gets the 'pod angle,' or he gets the 'first-degree pod angle,' or he gets a certain kind of lighting." We had a blue tinge around the gills and things like that. So even if you don't know who's a pod and who isn't, if you have the secret code, you can tell from the beginning.

AI: There are a lot of zoom shots in the film. When you zoom in, it's different from tracking: the space is flattened out because it's happening through the lens rather than moving through space. This seems so appropriate given the "flattening" of the characters. Was this a conscious decision that you, or Chapman, arrived at?

PK: It's something like that. I seldom like to use a zoom. I much prefer tracking and keeping that perspective with the background. But there was meant to be a kind of playfulness all the way through here, to set in motion a whole series of subliminal elements that we hope will add up to something. You have all the little telephone cords and dartboards that are swinging—an emphasis on details, because I think that's where paranoia finally rests: in the details.

AI: Talk about the sound track. In the opening sequence, for example, we hear the swings before we see Robert Duvall as the priest seated on the swings. The sound keys us in for what is about to happen. How did you elaborate that sound track? Was it in the script stage, or during filming, or after?

PK: Well, the sound was there in many cases before we went in to shoot the film. The taxi driver who takes them to the airport is Don Siegel, who had directed the original *Invasion*. And his wife was standing there as they got into the taxi, sort of blocking off some lights for us. And just as Kevin McCarthy is in the film, carrying it over from the original, I wanted to pay homage to Don, who is also a friend of mine. Just to digress for a moment, I really loved and respect the original film enormously and was worried about paying enough respect to it. Observant critics later, of course, said things like, "Well, obviously they didn't love the original the way I did, and they shouldn't have remade it." But we did try to respect the original and do a variation on a theme. I hesitated to call this a "remake" because, as with a piece of music, if you take a certain theme and then run it through with other variations, you can come up with something interesting.

To get back to the sound track and that scene where they're going through the tunnel. . . . Well, I live in San Francisco, and I was driving through there, and some motorcycles had come by. You only get the force of it hearing it on Dolby, but the idea of those motorcycles beginning at the back, swinging around, and then eventually ending up on surround speakers . . . it may be more commonplace now, but back then it really wasn't being done. And people weren't using the full range of the possibilities of Dolby. At the time that this film was made, Dolby felt that this was the best Dolby sound track, and I think they still use it to demonstrate certain things.

AI: In terms of casting, if my memory serves, this was the first acting part for Leonard Nimoy since playing Spock in *Star Trek*. Was that one of the reasons you wanted to cast him?

PK: For a brief period in my life, I was going to do the first *Star Trek* movie. Somebody had called me and said Paramount was going to do a small version for about three million dollars, and it was going to be a throwaway movie, basically, because of some small success of *Star Trek*. It was coming back, and they realized there were Trekkies and so forth. I was delighted to hear that, as I had seen it, and I thought there was a possibility to make not the *Star Trek* that was finally made but something quite different—the way *The Fugitive* was for TV, and they redid it in a different way with the basic theme. I wrote for seven months basically around Leonard Nimoy, and at the last minute, just two weeks before *Star Wars* came out and a couple of months before *Close Encounters*, someone high up at Paramount decided, and this is one of my favorite lines, "There's no future in science fiction." The project was cancelled. Anyone who has worked in the film business knows these feelings, and I had been developing two other projects, and one was *Body Snatchers*. I didn't know if it would ever get made or not; the other was a script my wife had written on Richard Price's book *The Wanderers*, which we'd been trying to do for years, and again the studio took a piece of paper out of the drawer and said, "There's no market for teenage movies." This was another era, and he had the figures to show that teenage movies just weren't successful. So I wasn't able to do either of these movies. And then Warner Brothers, who had developed *Body Snatchers*, decided they didn't want to do it, and United Artists said they wanted to do a low-budget movie on *Body Snatchers*, and the budget was about $2.9 million. And that's where Leonard Nimoy came from, my experience with *Star Trek*.

AI: Could you talk a little about how you conceived of the ending, and at what point did you let everyone know what it was going to be?

PK: The ending was stimulated from conversations I was having with Don Siegel about what happened with the original *Body Snatchers.* The studio had made them add bookends to the movie. He wanted to end it on a very scary note, but the studio added that little thing where they're going to call the FBI, and everything's going to be okay. And just at that moment, Kevin McCarthy popped his head into the office. I hadn't planned to use Kevin at that point, nor that theme of Kevin running for twenty years from movie to movie, trying to warn people that they're already here and bumping into the car in the middle of Donald Sutherland's joke. That wasn't in my mind, but Kevin came in and told me the same thing, that they had really wanted to make a harder-hitting movie the first time. So, we thought, "Let's try it with a real horror ending," where the only person, if there was ever going to be a sequel, would be Veronica Cartwright, who maybe could figure her way into the next movie.

In a way we have to find new kinds of heroes. There's a whole world that is coalescing around us, and we never know how to deal with it. We have all kinds of therapies and policemen, law and order, and we're always trying to figure out how to become heroes. But there's something in the idea that every man and every woman has to become a hero. That's what the Veronica Cartwright character is: she's alive, but absolutely terrified and horrified by things. If I were making a sequel, it would begin with her, with her being the bearer of the knowledge of what the "pod-ness" is—to spread the news that we can't go to sleep. That's sort of the metaphor of the piece, anyway: it's very easy to see fascism as something imposed by guys in uniforms, but every time it rises up, it is so readily received by people. Later they deny it, but Kennedy talked about that kind of thing—the dangers of conformity.

There were only three people who knew what the ending of the film was going to be: me, Rick Richter, and the producer. And we didn't tell any of the actors. The day before we shot it, we told Donald. We didn't know how people would respond. Donald could have said, "No way, man. I'm not a pod." But Donald being who he is, so bright and playful, he loved the idea. And then, right on the spot, we told Veronica Cartwright, and I never told the studio. They would call daily and say, "How are you gonna end this movie?" And I'd say, "Not telling." Fortunately, the movie was pretty successful, and so I was able to keep working.

AI: Did you keep it from the studio so that word didn't get out, or so that they didn't try to change your ending?

PK: Studios back then were populated by the types of guys who really think they have a gland in common with the public. They really believe that when they sit in an audience, they "get" exactly what the public wants. I've heard them say this. They don't talk about the gland, but they say, "You can trust me because I know what the audience wants." I mean, the history of big successes in the film industry has been the opposite of that. Not always, of course. But anyway, I was afraid of that. The guys at U.A., which later became Orion, were bright. They were more adventuresome people, and they let filmmakers make their movies. It was a great time, and they were a great company for that time. I don't know if anything quite like that exists now. Also, things weren't "pod-ized" quite as much in Hollywood then. The formulas weren't in place as much. There weren't guys going around giving lectures on character arc and things like that. In certain situations that kind of thing makes sense. The phrase "character arc" might be quite apt, but I remember talking to Tom Pollock, who was the head of Universal and a very bright guy. And "character arc" came up over a script I was working on. And I said, "Come on, in *Raiders of the Lost Ark* there's no character arc. Harrison Ford's character is essentially the same at the beginning as he is at the end. There's no development." He said, "No, that's not true." I said, "What do you mean?" He said, "Snakes. He fears snakes at the beginning, and at the end he confronts his own worst fear." We laughed about that, but it's a frustrating thing that all filmmakers go through. Maybe we can talk some time about the modern process of what film-makers go through in Hollywood: it's truly an industry now.

AI: You seem to have a foot in both worlds: you make studio films, but they are hardly typical of Hollywood. . . .

PK: I try not to think about all of that. I sometimes go to L.A. only once a year, you know, to go to the bank. Or sometimes, I'm not down there for years. I have a lot of friends there who are really bright, nice people. I lived there once for about six years. I began about thirty years ago in Chicago, trying to raise money for small projects, saying, "Hol-lywood's dead!" and giving all those standard speeches. And I ended up on contract at Universal a few years later, broken. When I did *Northfield*, I was making about $175 a week, and when I directed it—for about ten thousand dollars—I was sort of at the bottom of the barrel. But my philosophy is that I want to do things that interest me or amuse me, and to work with people who stimulate me as a director. I take a lot of time in casting, and I've been fortunate enough to work with wonderful actors. When I come to the set in the morning, I feel the director's job is not just to stimulate the actors or boss them around but to be stimulated by them, so that by the end of the day, I feel I've been greatly amused and interested. . . . This is our life, and this is what we do, and we're lucky to be doing it. I've been very fortunate somehow, despite many commercial failures, to keep going.

AI: I want to get back to *Body Snatchers*, if I may. My favorite scene is in Sutherland's kitchen, where he makes dinner. It feels so wonderfully natural, and almost improvised in the rhythms of cooking, eating, looking. How much of it comes from rehearsal? Or improvisation? Or is it basically scripted and done a few times until it feels right to you?

PK: Basically, it's scripted. Rick Richter, the screenwriter, was there the whole time. The film that we brought from Warner Brothers to United Artists was very different, and we began shooting about six weeks later. The scene was scripted, but you have to use the word "improvisation" in a certain sense. What it's about, what you're going for, it was already there. But the actors have to be comfortable, particularly in a scene like that, which is really about being human. It's a love story, really. So they have to find their humanity or their way into the scene. We rehearse for as long as it takes, and sometimes it takes a long time. But it's always rewarding when you're working with actors. I mean, Donald is an extremely bright man, and it's fun to see what he can put into a scene, and Brooke Adams too. I believe in a lot of rehearsals with actors. You can find out marvelous things from them.

AI: I'm guessing it's not in the script that Brooke Adams rolls her eyes?

PK: I asked her, "What can you do? Can you juggle, or what?" And she said, "Well, I can do this." If you notice when she does it, one eye goes this way, and the other goes that way, and it's an extraordinary thing. And I wanted to record that. I mean, I fell in love with her!

AI: I have a question about the peep show near the end of the film. Is the raunchy sex club part of the new society, or a remnant of the old one?

PK: That's interesting. That's right on the cusp of things on the edge of human society that can also be luring you into the pod society. That's the thin pornographic line. You should feel that it's a pod world they are being lured into. Those places are pretty scary anyway. In one of those bars a few years ago, a gangster was crushed to death. He was having sex with some girl on a piano, and it rose up and crushed him to death. I mean, you couldn't write anything like that. I assume it was a pod murder.

AI: You pioneered the NC-17 rating with *Henry and June.* Did you feel the NC-17 rating was a good or bad thing? Did it hurt you commercially? And how does that controversy now look to you?

PK: I don't think the film was an NC-17. I felt it adhered to the same standards as *Unbearable.* I guess it was because two women had sex, a little more than was insinuated in *Unbearable.* We were going to appeal. I mean, there are so many films where gratuitous sex is thrown around, where sex is treated obscenely, and I was angry. We decided not to appeal. The film went out and did great business wherever it was shown, in about 170 theaters, I think. And critics supported us. Then outside Boston, it was banned, and in the South they said, "NC-17 is just X disguised." And everybody supporting us disappeared and just walked away from the argument, from the NC-17 rating, and Blockbuster refused to stock it. And eventually it really hurt the movie. We could never go wider in terms of theaters, even though it was doing really good business where it was playing.

There were six scenes that gave us the rating, and I didn't want to get rid of them. It didn't feel right. One of them was the shot of the postcards at the beginning. I don't like censorship being used arbitrarily, and I do feel it was being used in that way. I guess I felt badly about some of the critics not continuing the fight.

AI: About *Rising Sun*—when you first read Crichton's novel, what attracted you?

PK: The whole sense of manipulation of images was one of the key things that really attracted me, and the Sean Connery character—the detective who uses the ancient Japanese methods to detect things, where things are not as they seem. I felt we could make a film that, instead of coming up with answers, could leave some questions at the end.

AI: What an exhilarating opening sequence, from the intense red, to the karaoke bar!

PK: That red in the opening is the sun, not exactly meant as symbol, more as representation: glare, intense heat, the place where our eyes are not supposed to look for fear of being blinded.

AI: When Eddie follows the blonde outside, titles of the date and time made me think of *Psycho*. . . .

PK: That's interesting, and I wish I had intended it. I love the idea that both films deal with voyeurism while being a murder mystery. I was thinking more of those Raymond Chandler films, brought out of their murky forties setting into the new, gleaming L.A. now on the Pacific Rim, where the savvy, world-weary wizened detective makes his way across a noir landscape through a complicated plot, revealing answers to some mysteries, unearthing others left unanswered. He teaches his fresh sidekick how to be constantly alert, aware, awake to every nuance and danger of the new world. And that edgy awareness—that heightened, paranoid apprehensiveness—is precisely what every voyeur craves. In the end, Wesley is left standing at her door, staring in: he has become a wise detective and a first-class voyeur.

AI: What's more, the music occasionally invokes that of Bernard Herrmann's scores for Hitchcock.

PK: Bernard Herrmann was certainly the master of the obsessive/thriller genre. Toru Takemitsu and I talked extensively about his approaches to underscoring a scene. In general, Toru preferred to be more spare in his music, believing that silence was eloquent, but I think I pushed him a bit into the Herrmann area. For me, it was important to have Japan's greatest composer create the musical atmosphere for the film. (Toru agreed with the film's point of view, which was later attacked as "Japan bashing.")

AI: Then again, maybe Truffaut is a more important inspiration for you than Hitchcock?

PK: When I started making films, I was very interested in what the New Wave was doing. Truffaut had done his first three movies, which just knocked me out. I shot this film *Goldstein* in 1963 in Chicago. And Truffaut happened to be in Chicago visiting a friend who was working on Arthur Penn's movie, and he came to the very first screening of *Goldstein*. I was absolutely thrilled. We had a party afterwards at Nelson Algren's apartment, and my wife went to him and said she loved *400 Blows, Shoot the Piano Player*, et cetera. And he was trying to tell us he was into something else now—shooting Hitchcock movies (laughs).

AI: *The Right Stuff* is a thrilling adaptation of a "nonfiction novel." How much contact did you have with Tom Wolfe while filming, and why did you choose to frame the movie with the Chuck Yeager episodes?

PK: I had almost no contact with Tom. We met once or twice at the beginning, but he really didn't want to be involved. He just said, "You make the movie." I spoke to him once or twice on the phone, and then we showed him the movie when it was finished, and he seemed to respond very strongly to it. He realized it was going to be tough to make a movie of the book.

For me, *The Right Stuff* was Chuck Yeager, but seeds he planted went into the others—when the individual becomes a group with the astronauts. That form of individual endeavor—it is heroism, but also something else called "the Right Stuff." The real Chuck Yeager was on set all the time, and the real guy won't drive over fifty-five miles an hour. He absolutely believes it's dangerous, and I'd drive by him, you know, giving him the finger on my way to work. But when it came to going through the skies, he was absolutely fearless. That was the right stuff. It begins with him, and it ends with him.

AI: What a rich sound track in *The Right Stuff*! Can you talk, for example, about the sound that accompanies the reporters?

PK: It's grasshoppers or locusts. It's an attempt to find a visual or audio correlation to some of Tom Wolfe's writing. We even created specific sounds for each rocket. And then we'd take the sound of the first rocket and add sounds to it, and so on. . . . As the rockets got bigger and bigger, so the baby sound is contained in the larger sound. We try to be playful with the sound tracks.

AI: Don't we hear the Inuit song from *The White Dawn* as John Glenn circles the earth?

PK: Yes. When I asked the old woman through an interpreter if she happened to know an old Eskimo song, she began to chant that fragile, melodic tune. And the old woman was joined in her incantations by Lou Gossett, Portagee, who tried to hum away his forlornness by joining her in her little song of succor. It became their fragile, doleful theme for a moment; then, as the entire tribe migrates, Mancini swells it into an epic, heroic suite.

Later, someone translated the words she was singing: "This man has asked me to sing something so I am just making this up and I hope that he likes what I am singing." In other words, she sings a kind of improvised nonsense, which in the course of its evolution in *The White Dawn* (and *The Right Stuff*) comes to convey emotion on an epic scale. From that little woman in the frozen north to John Glenn circling the world!

AI: You often use songs to anchor a scene . . .

PK: It's those little songs (like the ones we hum unconsciously in the shower) that get me every time: the Janacek folk song ("The Holy Virgin of Frydek"), which floats behind Binoche in *The Unbearable Lightness of Being*; the Wanderer's anthem that buoys the boys in the Bronx; the "Battle Hymn of the Republic" that John Glenn hums when he's plummeting to earth in a fireball, or the Marines' Hymn when he's masturbating, in competition with Dennis Quaid's Air Force Hymn.

AI: And how did you come up with the brilliant inclusion of "Mon Ami Pierrot" in *Quills*?

PK: It was by the oddest of Kunderian coincidences that I was looking at Du Maurier's "Trilby," where by chance I happened across "Mon Ami Pierrot." Yes, that very same little song is sung by the waif in the shadow of the guillotine, and picked up (subconsciously) by the Marquis, and becomes Sade's own little song of succor. Imagine: this most innocent of songs sung by these most innocent of children evolving into the creative mantra for this least innocent of men! Over the end credits, Warbeck includes it in his symphonic suite, where it is at once jaunty, mocking, and haunting.

AI: What motivates you to adapt a book into a movie?

PK: It varies. For example, I read *The Unbearable Lightness of Being* and loved it, but thought it would never make a movie. And I knew Milos Forman at the time. He was in San Francisco, and we would talk about Kundera's book, and he knew how much I loved it. About four months later, he called me and said, "Somebody wants to make a film of *The Unbearable Lightness of Being*. Would you be interested?" He couldn't make it because he had family in Czechoslovakia, and it would have been dangerous for them at that time. After I thought about it and went to Paris and spoke to Jean-Claude Carrière, it seemed possible that we could do a variation on the book. We could pull a linear story out of it rather than try to replicate the kind of musical structure Kundera has in the book.

There are some books you read, and you just want to see the movie of it. When I read *The Wanderers*, I thought I'd love to go back to that time with a movie.

AI: Because you want to share it with others?

PK: I think initially it's because I want to make it. I want to go in, and I think of music, or of an image, like Tereza coming to the door with a suitcase. Certain things start haunting me. Why do you want to make movies? I want people to share my feelings. I'm sure all filmmakers feel that way. I have to get obsessed. The one time I was under contract at Universal, they wanted me to do a lot of TV because they were paying me $175 a week, and they wanted me to earn that. And whenever I'd see the heads of the TV department coming, I'd hide in doorways—anything I could to avoid being cornered into doing things I didn't want to do.

We try, with varying degrees of success, to create and explore a world of beauty, mystery, sensuality—a world with its own rules, its own unique inhabitants. Characters, players, artists, clowns, jokers, and sometimes monsters—a world of fun. Fun while it lasted. Eventually each of these films had to bite the apple, to get released into that howling world where they journeyed through pain and suffering, often misunderstood, sometimes maligned. Yet when I look back on these films, they are now all suffused with a warm, golden glow of memory, green thoughts in a green shade. It makes me wonder if just outside the Garden of Eden someone had posted the sign: Beware all who enter here. You will be judged as to how you did at the box office.

Goldstein (1965)
USA
Producers: Philip Kaufman and Zev Braun
Directors: Philip Kaufman and Benjamin Manaster
Screenwriters: Philip Kaufman and Benjamin Manaster (inspired by Hasidic
    tales)
Cinematography: Jean-Philippe Carson
Editor: Adolfas Mekas
Music: Meyer Kupferman
Cast: Lou Gilbert (Old Man), Ellen Madison (Sally), Thomas Erhart
    (Scuptor), Benito Carruthers (Jay), Severn Darden (Doctor), Nelson
    Algren (Himself)
85 min.

Fearless Frank (a.k.a. *Frank's Greatest Adventure*; 1967)
USA
Producer: Philip Kaufman
Director and Screenwriter: Philip Kaufman
Cinematography: Bill Butler
Editors: Luke Bennett and Aram Boyajian
Music: Meyer Kupferman
Cast: Jon Voight (Frank), Monique Van Vooren (Plethora), Joan Darling
    (Lois), Severn Darden (Doctor and Claude), Anthony Holland (Alfred),
    Lou Gilbert (Boss), David Steinberg (Rat), Nelson Algren (Needles), Ben
    Carruthers (Cat)
83 min.

The Great Northfield Minnesota Raid (1972)
USA
Producer: Philip Kaufman (uncredited), for Universal Pictures
Director and Screenwriter: Philip Kaufman
Cinematography: Bruce Surtees

Editor: Douglas Stewart
Cast: Cliff Robertson (Cole Younger), Robert Duvall (Jesse James), Luke
    Askew (Jim Younger), R. G. Armstrong (Clell Miller), Dana Elcar (Allen),
    Donald Moffat (Manning), John Pearce (Frank James), Matt Clark (Bob
    Younger), Wayne Sutherlin (Charlie Pitts)
91 min.

The White Dawn (1974)
USA
Producer: Martin Ransohoff, for Paramount Pictures
Director: Philip Kaufman
Screenwriters: James Houston and Tom Rickman, based on Houston's novel
Adaptation: Martin Ransohoff
Cinematography: Michael Chapman
Music: Henry Mancini
Editor: Douglas Stewart
Cast: Warren Oates (Billy), Timothy Bottoms (Daggett), Louis Gossett Jr.
    (Portagee)
109 min.

Invasion of the Body Snatchers (1978)
USA
Producer: Robert H. Solo, for United Artists
Director: Philip Kaufman
Screenwriter: W. D. Richter, based on the novel *The Body Snatchers* by Jack
    Finney
Cinematography: Michael Chapman
Editor: Douglas Stewart
Music: Denny Zeitlin
Cast: Donald Sutherland (Matthew), Brooke Adams (Elizabeth), Leonard
    Nimoy (Dr. Kibner), Veronica Cartwright (Nancy), Jeff Goldblum (Jack),
    Art Hingle (Geoffrey), Leila Goldoni (Katherine), Kevin McCarthy (Dr.
    Miles J. Bennell), Don Siegel (Taxi Driver)
115 min.

The Wanderers (1979)
USA
Producer: Martin Ransohoff, for Orion Pictures
Director: Philip Kaufman
Screenwriters: Philip Kaufman and Rose Kaufman, based on the novel by
    Richard Price
Cinematography: Michael Chapman
Editors: Ronald Roose and Stuart H. Pappe
Cast: Ken Wahl (Richie), John Friedrich (Joey), Karen Allen (Nina), Toni
    Kalem (Despie), Alan Rosenberg (Turkey), Jim Youngs (Buddy), Tony

Ganios (Perry), Linda Manz (Peewee), William Andrews (Emilio), Erland
Van Lidth de Jeude (Terror), Dolph Sweet (Chubby Galasso)
113 min.

The Right Stuff (1983)
USA
Producers: Robert Chartoff and Irwin Winkler, for the Ladd Company
Director: Philip Kaufman
Screenwriter: Philip Kaufman, based on the book by Tom Wolfe
Cinematography: Caleb Deschanel
Editors: Glenn Farr, Lisa Fruchtman, Stephen A. Rotter, Tom Rolf, and
    Douglas Stewart
Production Designer: Geoffrey Kirkland
Special Visual Creations: Jordan Belson
Music: Bill Conti
Cast: Sam Shepard (Chuck Yeager), Scott Glenn (Alan Shepard), Ed Harris
    (John Glenn), Dennis Quaid (Gordon Cooper), Fred Ward (Gus Grissom),
    Barbara Hershey (Glennis Yeager), Kim Stanley (Pancho Barnes), Scott
    Paulin (Deke Slayton), Charles Frank (Scott Carpenter), Lance Henriksen
    (Wally Schirra), Veronica Cartwright (Betty Grissom), Pamela Reed
    (Trudy Cooper), Levon Helm (Jack Ridley/Narrator), Donald Moffat
    (Lyndon B. Johnson), Mary Jo Deschanel (Annie Glenn), Kathy Baker
    (Louise Shepard), Royal Dano (Minister), Jeff Goldblum (Recruiter),
    Harry Shearer (Recruiter), Scott Wilson (Scott Crossfield), David Clennon
    (Liaison Man)
193 min.

The Unbearable Lightness of Being (1988)
USA
Producer: Saul Zaentz
Director: Philip Kaufman
Screenwriters: Jean-Claude Carrière and Philip Kaufman, based on the novel
    by Milan Kundera
Cinematography: Sven Nykvist
Editor: Walter Murch
Cast: Daniel Day-Lewis (Tomas), Juliette Binoche (Tereza), Lena Olin
    (Sabina), Derek de Lint (Franz), Erland Josephson (The Ambassador),
    Pavel Landovsky (Pavel), Donald Moffat (Chief Surgeon), Stellan
    Skarsgard (The Engineer), Daniel Olbrychski (Interior Ministry Official)
171 min.

Henry and June (1990)
USA
Producer: Peter Kaufman, for Universal Pictures
Director: Philip Kaufman

Screenwriters: Philip Kaufman and Rose Kaufman, based on the book by
Anaïs Nin
Cinematography: Philippe Rousselot
Editors: Vivien Hillgrove, William S. Scharf, and Dede Allen
Cast: Fred Ward (Henry Miller), Uma Thurman (June Miller), Maria de
Medeiros (Anaïs Nin), Richard E. Grant (Hugo Guiler), Kevin Spacey
(Richard Osborn), Jean-Philippe Ecoffey (Eduardo Sanchez), Bruce Myers
(Jack)
134 min.

Rising Sun (1993)
USA
Producer: Peter Kaufman, for Twentieth Century Fox
Director: Philip Kaufman
Screenwriters: Philip Kaufman, Michael Crichton, and Michael Backes,
based on the novel by Michael Crichton
Cinematography: Michael Chapman
Editors: Stephen A. Rotter and William S. Scharf
Music: Toru Takemitsu
Cast: Sean Connery (Capt. John Connor), Wesley Snipes (Lt. Webster
Smith), Harvey Keitel (Lt. Tom Graham), Cary-Hiroyuki Tagawa (Eddie
Sakamura), Kevin Anderson (Bob Richmond), Mako (Yoshida-san), Ray
Wise (Senator Morton), Stan Egi (Ishihara), Stan Shaw (Phillips), Tia
Carrere (Jingo Asakuma), Steve Buscemi (Willy)
129 min.

China: The Wild East (1995)
USA
Producers: Xiao-zhen Jiang and Peter Kaufman, for Turner Original
Productions (TBS)
Executive Producer and Narrator: Philip Kaufman
Director and Screenwriter: Peter Kaufman
Cinematographer: Mitchell Farkas
Editor: Ruby Yang
Music: Tan Dun
96 min.

Quills (2000)
USA
Producers: Julia Chasman, Nick Wechsler, and Peter Kaufman, for Fox
Searchlight
Director: Philip Kaufman
Screenwriter: Doug Wright, based on his play
Cinematography: Rogier Stoffers

Editor: Peter Boyle

Music: Stephen Warbeck

Cast: Geoffrey Rush (Marquis de Sade), Kate Winslet (Madeleine LeClerc), Joaquin Phoenix (Abbé du Coulmier), Michael Caine (Dr. Royer-Collard), Billie Whitelaw (Madame LeClerc), Patrick Malahide (Delbené), Amelia Warner (Simone), Jane Menelaus (Renee Pelagie), Stephen Moyer (Prouix)

125 min.

Twisted (2004)

USA

Producers: Arnold Kopelson and Anne Kopelson

Coproducers: Peter Kaufman and Sheryl Clark, for Paramount Pictures

Director: Philip Kaufman

Screenwriter: Sarah Thorp

Cinematography: Peter Deming

Editor: Peter Boyle

Music: Mark Isham

Cast: Ashley Judd (Jessica Shepard), Samuel L. Jackson (John Mills), Andy Garcia (Mike Delmarco), David Strathairn (Dr. Melvin Frank), Russell Wong (Lt. Tong), Mark Pellegrino (Jimmy Schmidt)

97 min.

Hemingway and Gellhorn (2012)

USA

Executive Producers: Peter Kaufman, Trish Hoffman, James Gandolfini, and Alexandra Ryan, for HBO

Director: Philip Kaufman

Screenwriter: Jerry Stahl and Barbara Turner

Cinematography: Roger Stoffiers

Editor: Walter Murch

Music: Javier Navarrete

Cast: Clive Owen (Ernest Hemingway), Nicole Kidman (Martha Gellhorn), David Strathairn (John Dos Passos), Rodrigo Santoro (Zarra), Tony Shalhoub (Koltsov), Parker Posey (Mary Hemingway), Robert Duvall (Russian General)

A dramatic recreation of the romance between Hemingway and war correspondent Martha Gellhorn—as seen through her eyes—against the backdrop of the Spanish Civil War and subsequent international battles.

Accurso, Anthony. "Director's Cut." *Airpower* 33.6 (November 2003): 46–49.

Barra, Allen. "Historical Movies." *American Heritage* 55.6 (November/December 2004): 70.

Berman, Juliet. "Hall of Mirrors." Columbia University student essay, October 18, 2006.

Boyum, Joy Gould. "From an Epic of Adventure to Tragedy." *Wall Street Journal,* July 29, 1974, 8.

Carrière, Jean-Claude, and Philip Kaufman. "The Unbearable Lightness of Being." Unpublished screenplay, 2d draft, August 5, 1986.

Charity, Tom. *The Right Stuff.* London: British Film Institute, 1997.

Chute, David. "A Career Spent Near the Edge." *Los Angeles Times,* October 22, 2000, 1, 79–80.

Clements, Marcelle. "A Man for All Centuries, and Sins." *New York Times,* April 21, 2002, sec. 2, p. 1, 23.

Cowie, Peter. *Revolution! The Explosion of World Cinema in the Sixties.* London: Faber and Faber, 2004.

Dargis, Manohla. "Film Notes: Original Sinner." *Harper's Bazaar* 3468 (November 2000): 198.

Dempsey, Michael. Rev. of *The Great Northfield Minnesota Raid. Film Quarterly* 25.4 (Summer 1972): 47–49.

Ebert, Roger. Rev. of *The Right Stuff. Chicago Sun-Times,* October 21, 1983, 49.

Farber, Stephen. "Hollywood Maverick." *Film Comment* 15.1 (January/February 1979): 26–31.

Finney, Jack. *Invasion of the Body Snatchers.* New York: Simon and Schuster, 1998.

Frémaux, Thierry. "Fin août début . . . octobre." *Rue du premier-film: Programme de l'institut Lumière* 51 (August–October 2000): 3.

Fabbian, Davide. "Surveillance, Mystery, and Paranoia on the Barbary Coast." Columbia University student essay, April 29, 2010.

French, Philip. Rev. of *The Great Northfield Minnesota Raid. Sight and Sound* 43.1 (Winter 1973–74): 43–55.

Goodman, Walter. "This de Sade Savors Pen over Pain." *New York Times,* December 24, 2000, 20.

Goodwin, Michael. "Riding High with *The Right Stuff.*" *American Film* 9.2 (November 1983): 23–27.

Greenberg, James. "Say Anything." *Los Angeles* 45.11 (November 2000): 54–55.

Houston, James. *The White Dawn: An Eskimo Saga.* New York: Harcourt Brace Jovanovich, 1971.

Hunter, Stephen. "'Quills': The Sade Truth about Freedom's Price." *Washington Post,* December 15, 2000, C1:12.

Insdorf, Annette. "An Eye for an I: From Novels to Films." *Tin House* 2.2 (Winter 2001): 289–99.

———. "*Sun:* It's about Image." *New York Post,* July 31, 1993, 14.

———. "Team Players: Independent Filmmakers Popularize Ensemble Casts." *Washington Post,* January 14, 1996, G5.

Kael, Pauline. "The Current Cinema: Pods." *New Yorker,* December 25, 1978, 48, 50–51.

———. "The Current Cinema: Take Off Your Clothes." *New Yorker,* February 8, 1988, 67–70.

Kauffmann, Stanley. *A World on Film.* New York: Dell/Delta, 1966.

Kaufman, Philip. "The Right Stuff." Unpublished screenplay, n.d., Warner Bros. Entertainment.

———. "Rising Sun: From the Novel by Michael Crichton." Unpublished screenplay, April 21, 1992.

Kaufman, Philip, and Rose Kaufman. "Henry and June, from the Unexpurgated Diary of Anais Nin." Unpublished screenplay, 2d draft, July 25, 1989.

Knickerbocker, Paine. "When the Two Cultures Clashed, It Was a Matter of Survival." *San Francisco Chronicle,* July 28, 1974, Datebook.

Kundera, Milan. *The Unbearable Lightness of Being.* Trans. Michael Henry Heim. New York: Harper Perennial, 1999.

Lewis, Kevin. "Philip Kaufman: *Quills* and the Prickly Side of Free Expression." *DGA Magazine* 25.5 (January 2001): 19–21.

Lindroth, Colette. "Mirrors of the Mind: Kaufman Conquers Kundera." *Literature/Film Quarterly* 19.4 (October 1991): 229–34.

Mingst-Belcher, T'sera. "Mirrors and Windows, Lightness and Being." Columbia University student essay, October 21, 2004.

Mitchell, Sean. "Strangers in a Strange Land." *Premiere* 6.12 (August 1993): 58–63.

Mizejewski, Linda. "Dressed to Kill: Postfeminist Noir." *Cinema Journal* 44.2 (Winter 2005): 121–27.

Murray, Noel. Rev. of *Goldstein. A.V. Club,* January 25, 2006; accessed July 25, 2011. http://www.avclub.com/articles/goldstein,9416/.

Nin, Anaïs. *Henry and June.* From *A Journal of Love: The Unexpurgated Diary of Anaïs Nin, 1931–32.* San Diego: Harcourt, 1989.

Price, Richard. *The Wanderers.* Boston: Houghton Mifflin/Mariner, 1974.

Quills. Press kit. Fox Searchlight, 2000.

Rafferty, Terrence. "Adults Only." *GQ* (November 2000): 215–24.

Schwartz, Lauren. "Philip Kaufman's *Quills*: A Discourse on the Relationships between Creative and Sexual Repression and Expression." Columbia University student essay, January 2004.

Smith, Chris. "Auteur! Auteur! Filmmaker Philip Kaufman Is Almost Famous." *University of Chicago Magazine* 94.4 (April 2002): 35–39.

Smith, Gavin. "Heroic Acts, Subversive Urges." *Film Comment* 29.4 (July/August 1993): 36–39.

Sragow, Michael. "The Adventures of Philip Kaufman." *Sundance Film Festival Magazine* (1993): 32–37.

———. "Critics' Picks: New on DVD." *Baltimore Sun,* September 23, 2007, 3E.

———. "Fearless Phil." *San Francisco Examiner,* February 14, 1988, 13–14.

———. "The Return of the Marquis de Sade." *Salon.com,* July 27, 2000; accessed July 25, 2011. http://dir.salon.com/ent/col/srag/2000/07/27/quills/index.html.

Stack, Peter. "The Wanderers: 60s Innocence Lost." *San Francisco Chronicle,* June 21, 1996, D9.

Thompson, David. "A Filmmaker Both Promising and Forgotten." *New York Times,* September 10, 2000, sec. 2, p. 63.

Truffaut, François. *Les Films de ma vie.* Paris: Flammarion, 1975.

Twisted. Special Collector's Edition DVD, Paramount, 2004.

Ventura, Michael. "The Passions of Philip Kaufman." *San Francisco* 47.10 (October 2000): 86–91, 176.

Wells, Chris. "Adapting to the Surroundings: The Script to Screen Transformation of *The Unbearable Lightness of Being.*" Columbia University student essay, October 12, 2005.

Wilmington, Michael. "*Quills* Sees Sade as Rebel and Victim." *Chicago Tribune,* December 18, 2000, 1.

Wolfe, Tom. *The Right Stuff.* New York: Bantam Books, 2001.

Wright, Doug. *Quills and Other Plays.* New York: Faber and Faber, 2005.

———. "Quills." Unpublished screenplay, polished draft, fall 2000.

Zacharek, Stephanie. "The Race for Space Was Won with Gum." *New York Times,* May 11, 2003, 27.

Annette Insdorf is a professor of film studies at Columbia University, where she also directs the undergraduate film studies program. Her many works include *Francois Truffaut* and *Indelible Shadows: Film and the Holocaust.*

Books in the series
Contemporary Film Directors

The University of Illinois Press
is a founding member of the
Association of American University Presses.

Designed by Paula Newcomb
Composed in 10/13 New Caledonia LT Std
with Helvetica Neue LT Std display
by Barbara Evans
at the University of Illinois Press
Manufactured by Thomson-Shore, Inc.

University of Illinois Press
1325 South Oak Street
Champaign, IL 61820-6903
www.press.uillinois.edu